*smudging & incense-burning
essentials

smudging & incense-burning

essentials

cassandra eason

foulsham
LONDON • NEW YORK • TORONTO • SYDNEY

foulsham

The Publishing House, Bennetts Close, Cippenham, Slough, Berkshire, SL1 5AP, England

ISBN 0-572-02737-0

Cover illustration by Jurgen Ziewe

Printed in England by Cox & Wyman, Reading, Berkshire

Contents

Introduction

What is smudging?

The smoke from herbs has been central to magic and spirituality from ancient times. The burning of herbs both in their natural state and as incenses, mixed with a resin to create a rich, long-lasting stream of smoke, has been used in many cultures and ages to cleanse both physically and spiritually, as well as to make offerings to the deities. This burning or smoke ritual, also known as smudging, has recently re-entered the modern western world after centuries of decline, from the unbroken tradition of Native North American spirituality.

The herbs for smudging may be burned in various forms – the simplest is a bundle of dried herbs held together with twine, ignited at the end, blown out and allowed to smoulder. Loose dried herbs may be burned in a shallow dish that may contain sand or earth in the base. You can also burn very fine herbs or wood chips on a disc or cube of charcoal in a heatproof container.

Smudging also embraces burning incense and smudge sticks in rituals. Incense was originally used only in formal ceremonial rites, much as it survives today in our western religions. However, nowadays it has become available in floral fragrances and is on sale even in supermarkets, and is used both in quite informal rituals and simply to add a pleasant aroma to homes.

The smoke from aromatic oils can also be used for cleansing or empowering an area, but on the whole oils are not so versatile in ritual practices because it is not safe to move hot oil. For this reason, I have specifically not included oil-burning in this book. However, oils are a good way of gradually releasing and diffusing energies, using special burners, and the herb and incense meanings I give at the back of this book have the same significance as their equivalent oil fragrances.

The origins of smudging

Herbs have been used for healing and ritual since prehistoric times. Evidence dating back 60,000 years to the burial site of a Neanderthal man was uncovered in 1960 in a cave in the Zagros mountains in northern Iraq. Analysis of the soil around the human bones revealed large quantities of eight species of plant pollen, including yarrow and groundsel. All of these herbs are medicinal plants attributed with healing properties in modern herbalism.

Perhaps the best-known use of smoke in ceremony and worship is in the Native North American tradition, where it is offered to the spirits of nature and the cosmos, in particular to the Great Spirit and the creatrix, Grandmother Spider, who wove the web of the world and fashioned people from clay.

According to Hopi myth, Grandmother Spider fashioned animals and people from clay, cradling them in her arms while Tawe, Grandfather Sun, breathed life into them. Grandmother Spider continued to bring teaching to the different nations, returning in many forms. Indeed, some versions of Lakota myth tell that she came to them in a time of need as the shining, beautiful White Buffalo Calf Woman, or Wophe, who gave the men the sacred Lakota pipe with instructions how to smoke it as a focus for peaceful negotiation. Among the many other gifts she brought were the sacred plants necessary for smudging. She showed the women how to heal with smoke by burning sacred herbs in an abalone shell or a shallow bowl, and how to waft the fragrant smoke with a feather to keep their tepees and the whole encampment free from all harm.

Smudging in the modern world

It can be hard to adopt a practice that we feel is not our own, and our modern westernised society was largely shaped by industrialisation and the growth of the big city that broke the connection of people with the land.

However, before that our ancestors, too, would have burned herbs in their homes for cleansing and this practice still survives here and there, for example in the Scottish folk custom of burning juniper berries in the house on New Year's Day. So when you light a bowl of dried herbs or a smudge stick (a bunch of long herbs bound with twine), you are reaffirming our links with the folk traditions of an older world.

Smoke ritual is a powerful method of empowering places, artefacts and even yourself, as well as cleansing and removing negativity from your home and workplace, though the latter can be more difficult unless you can temporarily de-activate smoke alarms! You can smudge around the outside of buildings and around the boundaries of your property. You can psychically cleanse and empower the tools of your trade or letters or documents. I wonder now how I ever managed without my herbs, which are used just as frequently for practical purposes as magical ones (they work wonders for masking the smell of Mr Bear, my cat).

The purposes of smudging

Smudging can be either a ritual in itself or a prelude to a ritual. A circle of smoke or incense can be used to mark off a sacred space and enclose an area of power and protection in which to work.

Like any form of aromatic smoke ritual, smudging originated as a means of sending wishes and prayers into the cosmos and connecting the Earth plane to the spiritual beings there. And so today, it can be used to communicate with whatever spirit you believe in, whether you envisage a single God, or gods and goddesses, wise ancestors, spirit guides, guardian angels or the Native North Americans' Great Spirit. In addition, both the smoke and any words and actions that make up even a simple ceremony can create a state of altered consciousness as a light meditative state, enabling you to concentrate your thoughts.

Smudging connects Earth and Sky, both physically and spiritually. It can be quite eerily beautiful to see a single tendril of smoke rising upwards against a vivid sunrise or sunset or surrounded by a pool of candlelight. Even if you say not a single word, make no movement and use no other tool, you have created a magical space in the everyday world through which higher energies can penetrate and illuminate your consciousness.

At times when you need help, direction or healing, for either yourself or others, your smudging ritual can provide the vehicle for you to receive images or words in your mind – wise guidance from the universal well of wisdom that we can access at such moments.

The herbs ...

As I said earlier, herbs for smudging can be presented in various different ways, and some are easier to handle than others. While you are learning the art of smudging, you may find it easier to work with ready-prepared mixes or smudge sticks or plaited ropes. The most common herbs used in these are sage, cedar and sweetgrass, though you may also find lavender, thyme and bay mixes. The advantage of mixes is that they are likely to burn well, especially the large dried leaves of sage or cedar, making them ideal for smudging with a bowl – my own favourite method.

I would advise you to start by using a bowl of ready-prepared herbs. This frees you to concentrate on the most important aspects of smudging – purification, empowerment and healing – without worrying about such mundane matters as whether the herbs will light or keep burning. Once you are more practised and can tune easily into the psychic and spiritual aspects of the work, then you can take time to experiment with different herbs and smudges. Most suppliers of Native North American crafts and New Age stores sell smudge sticks and mixtures, and they are also easily obtainable by mail order and on the internet. I have listed a number of suppliers at the back of this book.

... and the smoke

Don't be put off smudging just because you hate the idea of smoke or smoking. You are not aiming to create a choking fog of smoke, but a single wisp, or two or three at the most, which can be directed for your purposes. In fact, during smudging, a room becomes very fragrant, especially if you use sweetgrass.

Even if you wish to cup or waft smoke over yourself as a cleansing ritual, you do not need to bring it too close to your nose or face or get it in your eyes. Unlike cigarette tobacco, the herbs we use for smudging do not contain tar to clog your lungs. But if you prefer, you can smudge with the doors and windows open, or even out of doors, although in practice the natural ventilation of a house is usually adequate.

Precautions

As with any fire, you should not leave your burning smudge stick or herbs unattended. I sometimes wedge a smudge stick in a broad-based candle-holder to fragrance a room, but you should place a metal tray underneath in case any of the burning material falls off.

Ready-prepared smudge sticks are usually well made and tightly tied, so they should not fall apart – again this is a good reason for buying commercial ones initially.

It is best to avoid smudging on a carpet or near furniture because of the risk of fire or burns. I always have a wet tea towel or a metal lid handy for quick dousing in case of accidents. While spiritually it is said not to be good practice to extinguish smudging materials with water (you leave them to go out or smother the flame), in an emergency you can use a bowl of water to dowse any over-enthusiastic stick. However, the more usual problem is keeping the sticks alight! Never douse oil or wax with water.

Remember, fire needs fuel, heat and oxygen to burn, so if you cut off one of these quickly, any problems can be avoided.

Keep smudging materials away from pets (one of my cats likes to eat the ash) and allow children to smudge only under very close supervision.

As you become more confident, security and precautions will become largely unconscious and spontaneous. Used sensibly, smudge sticks are no more dangerous than candles or incense and much safer than oil-burners. They have become part of my domestic world – which, at the time of writing, is still entirely unscorched.

Special cases

If you are pregnant you should take advice from a doctor or medical practitioner before using smudging as a part of any ritual. Check with a qualified herbalist, as a number of herbs should be avoided in any form especially during the first three months of pregnancy. I have given a list below. You will see that this includes the most popular smudging materials, i.e. cedar, sage and thyme. Rose petals, lavender and chamomile flowers burned at distance or out of doors should be quite safe but you should avoid inhaling the smoke and vapours.

The following herbs should not be inhaled or taken internally in pregnancy:

Aloe vera, angelica, anise, autumn crocus, barberry, basil, bay, caraway, cayenne, cedar, elder, fennel, feverfew, golden seal, hyssop, juniper, male fern, mandrake, parsley, pennyroyal, poke root, rosemary, rue, sage, southernwood, tansy, tarragon, thuja, thyme, wintergreen, wormwood, yarrow.

This is not a comprehensive list, however, so as with any substance you use in pregnancy check with a herbalist or pharmacist before taking them, especially in the early months of pregnancy. There are also medical conditions that warrant care with specific herbs. For example, avoid angelica if you have diabetes, ginger if you have high blood pressure, and rosemary if you have epilepsy or heart disease.

Babies and very small children and asthmatics should also avoid indoor smudging, as should anyone with lung problems.

How does smudging work?

The fragrances in smudging change our normal energy patterns, helping us to become more in touch with ourselves and the natural world. By bringing about these changes on a spiritual level, smudge sticks, herbs and incense used as the focus of a ritual can bring us into harmony with higher energies. The act of choosing and lighting the fragrance, and focusing on an intention, a need or an expression of praise or joy, brings blessings into our life, either intangibly or as an actual positive event or unexpected gift. Most importantly, whatever the purpose of the ritual, it can galvanise our inner powers, giving us a physical or mental kickstart, perhaps boosting our immune system or our determination to make positive practical changes in our everyday world.

Smudging is in itself an exchange of energies in which certain plants offer themselves for our healing and purification. We accept these health-giving properties, power or protection from them and in turn use the smoke from burning them as a way of contacting higher dimensions to amplify these blessings.

Recent research into the auras of plants and humans found that the electromagnetic fields of living organisms interact with and affect one another, far beyond the physical confines of the body, through the aura.

An aura is the field of psychic energy that surrounds all beings. It is believed to be created by the interaction of natural magnetic and electro-chemical reactions, combined with the energies of the subtle or spiritual forces within the body. Because this energy is not static, but interactive, the aura reflects not only the essential person but also his or her current emotional state. In certain circumstances, an aura can actually be seen as a coloured ellipse surrounding the person.

By hooking them up to electronic equipment, researchers have discovered that plants respond intensely to the thoughts of people in their environment. The death or threat of death to living cells, whether human, plant or animal, causes violent electromagnetic reactions in plants that were not personally threatened.

This does not mean you should not use herbs, but rather that you should honour the willingness of the plant to be used. If you pick one and it is very resistant, leave it as it is not ready to let go. When you have used some herbs, you can complete your side of the sacred bargain by planting other herbs or, more importantly, by working even in a small way towards preventing deforestation or the destruction of wetlands or helping to increase plant life in urban areas. When picking herbs, leave enough in the clump for re-growth and, when growing them, be especially cautious about the use of pesticides on the soil.

Smudging in individual and group rituals

Smudging is a good prelude to almost any kind of ceremony; many Native North American practitioners are surprised that when we carry out healing or therapeutic work, we do not smudge before and afterwards. Smudging is an excellent unifying exercise, whether for a group of friends, for family gatherings or with an individual with whom you wish to strengthen spiritual or emotional connections or perhaps to heal a rift. Believe me, the most critical relative can be silenced when you set fire to the bay leaves at Sunday lunch!

You can perform smudging as an individual or as a group of people joining together for an ecological project, to join the individual to the collective psyche. This can be especially useful for focusing energies on a collective need such as healing an absent person or perhaps sending positive energies to a war-torn place or an endangered species. If you want to create a physical sacred space, one person can smudge a clockwise circle around those who are gathered together.

An introductory smudging ritual

I describe the process of smudging in great detail in the next three chapters, but for now I shall give a brief explanation of the simplest form of smudging to use for group work so that you can begin straight away. The best way of learning smudging is by doing it and in the process developing your own unique way of working.

You can adapt the following ritual for solo use: carry out all the stages yourself but, instead of passing the bowl round, place it on a table or plinth and then hold it when you are making different affirmations of positive intention. If working alone, you could smudge a picture or place that is the focus of the ritual while naming the positive attributes and your hopes for the subject.

Arrangements for the ritual

Traditionally an abalone shell is used in smudging rituals of this kind. This is a shell lined with mother-of-pearl and has a number of tiny natural perforations to distribute the air evenly and give a regular stream of smoke. However, any dish-like open shell or ceramic heatproof dish will do. I have a flat, wide pottery dish with feet, marked with a spiral, which is particularly suitable as it has a lip to hold so that it can be carried or passed around.

For your first smudge, you might like to buy the large sage or cedar leaves that are ready-dried specifically for smudging. I found packets of similar large dried thyme leaves in a supermarket near St Malo in Brittany recently, but they are quite difficult to obtain in Britain.

You can put a layer of sand or soil in the bottom of the dish holding the herbs, if you wish, for safety and to stop the bowl getting too hot.

Herbs do frequently go out after being lit (cedar is especially prone to this). Practise lighting a bowl of herbs in advance so that the logistics do not interfere with the spirituality of the ritual. Use a small fan to fan the herbs and keep them alight.

Keep a lighted candle in the centre of your circle, ready for re-lighting, if necessary. Use a taper from the candle, as candle wax dripped on herbs does not help burning. If you make a positive affirmation as you re-light the flame, this can become part of the ritual, rather than being a distraction.

* Sit in a circle – you can work with just one or two other people if necessary and pass the bowl from one to the other in turn.

* Light a few herbs in the centre of the bowl or shell and wait until the flame becomes a glow. Fan the glow with your hand or a large feather, again as part of the ritual, saying:

Glow fire, grow smoke, carry these our positive intentions from the Earth to the Skies where they may be transformed into healing and power, joy and light.

* Cast a circle of smoke clockwise around the group. Begin in the East, the direction of the rising Sun, and walk round the perimeter of the circle of people saying:

I dedicate this circle to only good intent. May power and protection reside within it.

* Fan the bowl and speak words concerning the topic of the ritual, whether this is an environmental or a personal issue.

* Pass the bowl and the fan to the person sitting immediately to your right. They can fan the smoke and add their thoughts.

* Continue in this way, passing the bowl and adding words of encouragement or wisdom, until the bowl returns to you. The positive energies of the words will be amplified by the fragrant smoke. If the dish or shell becomes hot, place it in a large dish or deep tray filled with sand or earth. Children can, with help, speak their words over the bowl; this can be good if you are merging two families together or there have been family sorrows. If little ones are around, do not waft the smoke.

* Thank the benign spirits of the universe and the wise ancestors and leave the bowl to burn in the centre while the group enjoys a simple meal prepared beforehand.

A ritual to welcome a new family member

This is an actual ritual that worked in welcoming Julie, a 14-year-old girl who, with her father Colin, moved into the home of Anne and her own pre-teenaged children, Dean and Stuart. Julie hardly ever saw her birth mother, Sarah, who lived abroad, and she was feeling very insecure as her father, who had devoted all his attention to her for a number of years, was away.

Anne carried out a ritual on another day to welcome Colin as her new partner and they had some private smudging ceremonies to strengthen their personal connection and to take away resentment.

On this occasion, many of Anne's other relatives were present to share the ceremony.

✳ Anne lit and fanned the bowl, saying:

I welcome Julie into this family. I have already come to love her sense of humour, her kindness when any of us is sick or worried, the fabulous curries she makes, the way she defended Dean when he was being bullied in the park and her willingness to overlook my bad temper in the early morning, which I am trying to improve.

✳ Then she passed the bowl and the fan to the person sitting on her immediate right, her mother Elaine. Elaine fanned the bowl and said:

I am so pleased to have a granddaughter at last. I welcome Julie and her lovely singing and dancing that fill me with joy. I appreciate the wonderful way she walks my dog Ciao who loves her dearly too, the way she fixes my hair when it is a mess and her patience when I don't understand her music.

* Each person in the circle – aunts, uncles and new step-in-laws –
  took a turn to say a few words. When it was Julie's turn she also
  mentioned what she liked about her additional family.

Since negativity is forbidden at a ceremony like this, the exercise is
valuable in highlighting the positive aspects of a situation that none of
the people present might have chosen, but which hold great potential
for a strong and happy future together. Anne also held ceremonies for
her own children so they were not left out, and each was followed by
a special meal. When the herbs were burned through, the family buried
them in the garden and planted a lavender bush, Julie's favourite.

Chapter 1
Traditional smudging

S mudging, or smoke ritual, has gradually evolved over thousands of years, embracing the practices and beliefs of people from widely differing cultures. Inevitably, therefore, in its most developed form, it may involve complex ceremonial practices using special tools and accompanied by esoteric chants.

But its origins are very simple; you need nothing more than herbs to make the smoke and your bare hands to fan it. You do not even require a great knowledge of the huge variety of herbs available. (I have given a list of just 65 in Chapter 11, but there are literally dozens more. If you want to study them in more detail, see the books listed on page 182.)

The traditional herbs for smudging

Just three herbs form the basis of Native North American smudging: cedar, sweetgrass and sage. These three are so versatile that you could carry out almost any smudging ritual without the need for any other herbs. For this reason, I have devoted this chapter to describing their properties in detail, ending with two rituals for you to practise.

The herbs may be burned loose, in a bowl or other suitable heatproof container, on a charcoal block, or bound into smudging sticks. All of these methods are described fully later in the book.

Two varieties of sage are particularly popular: California White Sage *(Salvia apiana)* and Western Grey Sage *(Artemisia tridentata)* from Oregon. I have given the generic names for these as I know they work so well. But there is a wide variety of similar sagebrush plants, usually growing in desert places or on mountains in North America and increasingly in Australia. These are related to the culinary sage that we know in Britain, but are much broader-leaved. Desert sages are used in ready-prepared smudge sticks and herbs, which, as I said in the introduction, you may find easier to work with initially, while you explore the many uses of smudging both in your everyday world and in ritual.

Most practitioners agree that white and grey sage are the best smudge materials as both burn well without charcoal, do not need constant re-lighting and do not fall apart when burned as a smudge stick. They can also be used in absolutely any ceremonial or personal work since they have both cleansing and empowering effects. Grey sage is especially associated with women and is used for house clearance and space clearance, while white sage is used for purification of the self on personal spiritual journeys. It is also good for ceremonies of all kinds, being used in, for example, the modern Sun Dance of power and healing that is still held at the beginning of August by a number of Native North American clans. These people also give smudge sticks as special gifts when visiting Elders or a Medicine Man or Woman, in the same way you might take a bottle of wine when visiting a European household, though a smudge is a very special sacred gift.

Smudging herbs are almost always used dried, though some practitioners do mix a few fresh sprigs with the dried. You can use a herb alone, or two or three mixed in a bowl. Alternatively, you may use them in sequence, for example, first cedar to cleanse and protect, followed by sage for further purification and power, and finally sweetgrass to bless and heal. But as I said, since the broad-leaved sages have both purifying and empowering energies, they can be substituted for either cedar or sweetgrass.

Sage: Transformation and empowerment

California white, or desert, sage has broad leaves and so is easy to burn loose in a bowl or in a stick. It has a stronger fragrance than the western grey sage. But, as I said earlier, there is a wide variety of sages from different regions of America and Canada and similar herbs are grown in the desert regions of Australia; these are all very widely obtainable. You can make smudge sticks of culinary sage but, unless you can get large dried clumps, you may find it easier to burn this on charcoal in a bowl.

Sage drives away all darkness and replaces it with powerful positive feelings. Negative energies are carried upwards on the smoke and are transformed, falling as healing sunbeams.

Sage will energise where there is stagnation or exhaustion. It will trigger the innate power of the body, mind and soul for regeneration. Nicholas Culpeper, the sixteenth-century English herbalist whose book is still in print today, said: 'Why should a man who has sage in his garden ever die?'

Sage will clear and focus the mind, so smudging with sage is good when preparing for examinations or learning, or for increasing psychic power. Sage leaves and branches are traditionally wrapped around sacred objects to keep them from harmful influences and from losing power.

White sage is also good for cleansing and empowering the human auric field and crystals. It can be a good herb to burn to mark the beginning of your special time for spiritual work and you can cast a smoke circle around yourself to create boundaries and concentrate power.

Sage is very easy to burn and keep alight, either as a stick or in a bowl.

Cedar: Cleansing and protection

The cedar used in smudging is usually Western Red Cedar or California Incense Cedar. Thuja, the generic name for cedar, means 'sacrifice'. Cedar is used in smudge sticks or bundles, but the loose tips or needles can also be burned in a bowl if dried first. By needles, we mean the long green brush of leaves and not, as I used to think, the tiny needles of the kind that are shed by Christmas trees. The wood chips need charcoal (see Chapter 2) to help them burn well.

Cedar is a herb of purification, protection and healing and is a good herb for the home and for protecting tools and special belongings.

People of the north-west American Indian nations used whole cedar branches to cleanse a tepee, making sweeping movements through the air with them. Burning cedar is equally effective for us, especially when you move to a new home.

Cedar is called the prayer incense, because on its smoke it carries invocations to Grandmother Spider for the removal of pain and sorrow from yourself or others and for keeping sickness and unhappiness away from the home. You can of course call upon your own personal healing deity or angel when using it.

Cedar has a more subtle scent than sage but, since it is sometimes difficult to keep alight if your stick is even slightly damp, I would begin smudging with sage.

Sweetgrass: Positive energies, gentleness and healing
This is my own personal favourite and has such a gentle sweet fragrance; it is loved by children and anyone who finds sage overpowering.

Sweetgrass is called the hair of the Earth Mother, or Holy Seneca, or vanilla grass. It grows naturally in long strands, which are frequently braided or plaited together in the fields as soon as it is picked and so contains very concentrated Earth energies. The strands can also be bought separately, and some people prefer to buy them like this and plait their own braids, using the opportunity to focus on the healing powers of the herb.

Sweetgrass is the herb of the Mother Goddess, who in many indigenous cultures plays an important role as creator and nurturer of people, plants and animals.

The Mother Goddess concept is a universal one and was the first focus of worship from palaeolithic times. With the coming of patriarchal religion in the second millennium BC, the Mother Goddess became the wife of the Father God – or disappeared entirely – and in Christianity she became the Virgin Mary. In Native North American tradition she had several guises, appearing most frequently as Grandmother Spider. She was also the Corn Mother, who gave nourishment to humankind and acted as wise teacher to the tribes.

Sweetgrass therefore has a special significance to women and the concept of female deity, and it naturally attracts the health-giving power and abundance of the Mother figure, whether you think of her as the Corn Mother, Grandmother Spider or your own goddess figure to whom you relate. Women sometimes find that they explore their spirituality best by using this herb alone, as it does have purifying properties, although these are quite subtle. Some practitioners find that grey sage serves a similar function.

To smudge with sweetgrass, light one end of a braid and gently waft it or place the braid in a flat heatproof dish. It may look as if it is not alight, because it smoulders very slowly.

Ask for whatever it is you need, smudging first over your head, then your heart, followed by your navel and finally the womb or genital area. This is especially potent when done outdoors in the sunshine, though you must be careful not to allow sparks to fall on dry grass.

Try sitting with your dish of smoking sweetgrass by candlelight or moonlight; you can ask for beauty and blessings to enter your life, and relax as you absorb the magical fragrance, allowing light to enter your very being. You can visualise the smoke being transformed into silver light and inhale this very gently through your nose, exhaling darkness through your mouth, equally slowly and gently.

Sweetgrass is protective and unburned sweetgrass braids or bundles are traditionally hung over doorways and entrances.

Sweetgrass can also be wrapped around special objects when they are not in use.

Empowering your herbs

Whatever method you use to burn your smudging herbs – in a home-made or ready-prepared smudge stick or placed in a bowl – you can add to their natural properties by endowing them with power in a short ritual.

In this empowering ritual, we will use the four main compass points – North, East, South and West – plus the directions of up and down. This tradition translates well into the magical practices of any culture, and makes magical work instantly three-dimensional. The six directions are the basis of the Native North American Medicine Wheel, which we shall examine more closely later.

Arrangements for the ritual

If you are using a smudge stick, hold it between your hands. If you are using a bowl, place your herbs in it and hold this during the ritual.

Stand so that there is space round you and visualise a circle of fire with yourself in the centre. If you wish, light a circle of red candles.

* First face the East, the direction of dawn and spring. Raise your stick or bowl and say:

Golden light streaming from the East, power of dawn, brightness of morn, fill these my sacred herbs with clarity and vision.

* Turn next to the South, the direction of noon and summer. Lift your smudge stick or bowl upwards and say:

Blazing fires of the South, brilliance of noon and rippling fields of golden ripening grain, fill these my sacred herbs with inspiration and nobility of purpose.

✳ Face the West, the direction of dusk and autumn, and raise your smudge tools once more, saying:

Oceans and rivers of the West, final blazing glory of long days ended and the first star of evening, fill these my sacred herbs with love and healing.

✳ Now, face the North, the direction of midnight and winter. Lift your stick or bowl, and say:

Rocks and mountains of the North, snows and enveloping velvet darkness that bring rest and gentle contemplation, fill these my sacred herbs with compassion and wisdom of the ancestors.

✳ Standing in the centre of your visualised fire circle, lift your stick or bowl high in the air. Say:

Father Sky, bless these sacred herbs, empower them to overflowing with thrusting vitality and joyfulness.

✳ Finally, lower your herbs towards the ground and press down with your feet, saying:

Mother Earth, bless these your own herbs and us your children, endowing them and us with protection and connection with all life, herb and human, flower and animal, insect and bird, crystal and stone.

As well as charging your herbs with power, you can create a complete ritual by facing and invoking the six directions with your smudge and then smudging yourself (see pages 91–2) as a means of empowerment or protection.

A three-herb ritual to cleanse your home

This ritual is a good example of the way you can use three smudging herbs in succession. If you combine all three herbs in a bowl, fan the smoke first anti-clockwise (this direction is always used to remove negativity) followed by clockwise (the direction used to restore positive energies). You can combine the empowerment of the herbs with the ritual.

In larger-scale ceremonies, sage, the most powerful herb, is often burned first, and its fragrance continues working while cedar is introduced to drive out any remaining negativity and bring healing. Finally, sweetgrass gently uplifts and adds abundance and spiritual blessings to the empowering sage.

However, as I suggested earlier, it is equally valid to begin with cedar, the cleanser, followed by sage to purify and empower and finally the 'Good Fairy' sweetgrass in a natural progression.

The choice is yours. As you smudge more and your confidence grows, together with your knowledge and experience, you may wish to try other combinations. You can use all three of the herbs suggested here or indeed any other mixture of cleansing and empowering herbs – choose from the list on pages 72–7.

This ritual is especially good for major purification, perhaps of a house after a quarrel, and for personal smudging if you or a loved one has been subject to malice or hostility. It will remove all kinds of anger, sorrow and bad luck.

Arrangements for the ritual

Before you begin, you must locate the 'heart' of your home. By this I mean not the actual physical centre, but the place where the family gathers to relax or eat. Alternatively you can work on a patio, in a yard or garden and draw a circle in smoke, standing in the centre to represent the heart of the home.

Make sure you work well away from electrical appliances and delicate fabrics.

* Light a bowl of sage in the centre of the room or circle and honour in turn the six directions.

* Face each of the six directions in turn, beginning in the East and turning clockwise as you did in the empowering ceremony, saying for each direction:

> *Light, life, loveliness, abundance, descend from above,*

rise from below.

* Return to the centre and repeat the chant for the upward and finally the downward direction.

* Leave the bowl of sage burning in the centre of the room or circle. From a candle, light a taper and then a cedar smudge stick. (I recommend using a taper, because if you use a candle to light herbs you can inadvertently drip wax on them. If the cedar goes out, re-light it as part of the ritual.)

* Face the East once more. Beginning with the left-hand corner in front of you, visit the four corners of the room, working to the right and ending with the left-hand corner behind you. Smudge three anti-clockwise circles in each corner, saying for each:

> *Darkness flee hence,*
> *Blessed be.*

* Return to the centre and raise your stick to make three large anti-clockwise circles above your head, saying:

> *Above and around,*
> *Peace surround.*

* Next lower the stick, kneel and make three anti-clockwise circles round you, saying:

> *Below and around me,*
> *Light and harmony.*

* Finally, light the sweetgrass braid with the taper and, holding it at the bottom and about a third of the way up to support it, again face the East. Working clockwise, go to the four corners of the room,

this time beginning with the right-hand corner behind you and ending in the right-hand corner in front of you. Say in each corner as you make a single clockwise circle:

Light, life, loveliness, abundance, enter and forever be.

* Return to the centre and greet the Sky and the Earth with the same blessing.
* Place the smudge sticks in large, broad, fireproof dishes on a metal tray in the centre and allow them and your sage to burn through.
* Open any doors and windows. Be careful when tidying up afterwards as the holders can get very hot.

Chapter 2
The Materials and Methods of Smudging

Smudging equipment can be as elaborate or simple as you wish. We have already seen that smudging can be carried out with just three common herbs, placed loose in a bowl, with the smoke fanned by your bare hands. However, many people like to add a little more ceremony to their rituals. You may like to obtain a specially crafted fan and an ornate, flat dish for burning herbs and keep them wrapped in a leather bundle or bag with sage or sweetgrass to protect them. (On the other hand, you may prefer to make smudging part of your everyday world, using your kitchen dishes and raiding your container of dried chamomile tea when you want to smudge.)

In your rituals, there is no reason while you should not have a mixture of the beautiful and the practical. On some occasions you may wish to smudge with your special tools under the full moonlight or at dawn to celebrate the unity of all creation and perhaps ask for help for a species or nation under threat. On others, for example if you are expecting visitors, you may only have time to whisk round the house with a purifying smudge stick as you might with a vacuum cleaner, especially if you know there may be underlying tensions or very different world views.

If you are going to smudge regularly – and safely – it is probably a good idea to start gathering together some items that you will keep specially for your rituals. Again I have to say that this does not mean expensive or special tools. My most valuable piece of equipment for smudging with charcoal (see also Chapter 4) is a pair of barbecue tongs, quite the safest and most effective tool I have found for holding a disc of charcoal while lighting it. Over the next few pages, we shall look at the items of equipment you will most need.

Smudging bowls

As I said in the Introduction, traditionally, the Native North American Indians used abalone shells to hold their herbs for smudging. Shells are symbolic of the Mother Goddess and their use completes the combination of all four elements in the ritual – the shell representing Water, Earth in the form of the dried herbs, Fire in the glowing herbs and Air in the smoke. However, even dried herbs contain some water and so can be regarded as representing the element Water if you choose not to use a shell. Through this melding of all four elements, the smudging thereby creates a fifth, Ether or Spirit, and it is this energy that lifts the ritual from the mundane to the magical plane and in turn helps to create the impetus to transform dreams and desires into actuality.

A flameproof bowl of almost any kind can be substituted for the shell. My own favourite smudging bowl is ceramic, broad and quite flat with a shallow rim, a wide lip that remains cool even when herbs are heated and broad feet so it can be placed on a table or floor without risk of scorching. It has raised spirals inside, a symbol that in all cultures since palaeolithic times has represented the Earth Mother.

You could make your own and glaze it, endowing it with personal energies.

If you use a broad, shallow bowl, you can place burning charcoal discs or small blocks in the centre and smoulder flowers or herbs round the edges of the charcoal as well as directly on it. However, I would not really recommend walking around with burning charcoal unless it is in an enclosed container – it is extremely difficult to deal with if it falls out. I would suggest you look at some images and descriptions of a variety of burning dishes and if possible go not only to New Age stores but also to potteries and hardware shops, as once you get the right herb burner, smudging become so much easier.

You may also want to find a container suitable for holding smouldering smudge sticks for lengthy periods of time, for example when you are cleansing a room over a period of hours if the vibes are really bad, or when you do not want to hold it in a ritual. Most of the smudge stick will need to be outside, and a vase with a handle and a broad base is a good investment.

You also need a deep bowl for sand or earth in which you can extinguish smudge sticks at the end of a ritual, if they have not gone out naturally. You may also stand your vase of smudge sticks in this, to catch the ash or any sparks.

Charcoal

Loose herbs, as opposed to herbs tied into bundles or smudge sticks, can be burned on charcoal. Charcoal is considered a gift from Mother Earth and was used frequently in the Native North American world. Its colour is a natural absorber of negative energies and as it forms ash so the redundant energy is transformed into Fire energy. Charcoal can be bought in discs or briquettes, and is readily available from New Age shops and even hardware stores. Burn them in a special censer or flat dish with a layer of sand or earth. Do not use an abalone shell as a container when burning with charcoal, because the heat might crack it.

The easiest charcoal to work with initially is an individual disc about the size of a very large coin. This will have an indentation in the centre on which you can scatter your petals or herbs. You can burn any herb or flower on charcoal, where it will smoulder and allow the fragrance to be gently released. If you do have problems when trying to burn directly any of the herbs I suggested above, charcoal is a sure winner.

Unless you were an exemplary Scout or Girl Guide, however, you will probably find that charcoal discs and blocks, like barbecues, can be incredibly difficult to light at first without burning yourself. Practice, I'm afraid, is the only solution.

Using charcoal for burning

The very easiest way to ignite a disc is to light a long cook's match or taper. Pick up your charcoal in barbecue tongs and light it over a censer or dish, placed on a metal tray or on the ground. Light one edge of the disc and place it in the censer. It is sometimes hard to tell if charcoal is alight initially, as it may still look dull, but do not touch it as it will be extremely hot even if it has gone out. Blow or fan gently and you may see a glow.

The block will slowly turn greyish white when it is at the right heat for burning your herbs. This may take about 15 minutes, so allow plenty of time before your ritual. There are faster burning charcoals, but you may find that this initial preparation time away from the world does enable you to meditate quietly. You can light a sage smudge stick or a frankincense or sandalwood incense stick while you wait for the charcoal to heat – this will help you to transfer your energies from the mundane world to the spiritual plane.

When the charcoal is white-hot, drop just a few herbs at first in the centre of the disc, adding grains gradually as part of the ritual. In some forms of charcoal you can see the fire crackling but the principle is the same. For group rituals you can use larger censers and blocks, or even a barbecue, and drop your herbs on to the smouldering coals.

You can add herbs to the charcoal gradually throughout the ritual, asking that the powers and protection be increased.

Fans

The purpose of a smudging fan is to spread the smoke from a bowl of herbs around the person, object or place to be cleansed. They also assist in cleansing the human aura or psychic energy field. Obviously, you can use your hands to fan the smoke, but traditionally the Native North Americans used feathers and wing fans, which were believed to add the qualities of the particular bird to the magic. Below I have listed some of the properties associated with each of the different birds.

For a number of people in the modern world, using feathers or a bird's wing – even one found naturally – feels unnatural or even unpleasant. If you prefer, you can visualise your chosen bird as you use your hand or a leafy twig to fan the herbs. There are also many beautiful and more conventional fans available in junk shops, for example, the kind Victorian and Oriental ladies used to stave off the vapours when faced with an indelicate remark from an insensitive beau.

You can fan your bowl with a single large feather, ideally one you find yourself on a shore or in a field. However, wild-bird parks and sanctuaries often sell a variety of beautiful feathers and you can choose the right size and shape from these. You can also bind a number of feathers together on a band.

Mail-order outlets of Native North American crafts and New Age shops often sell traditional turkey-feather fans. Some of these can be quite elaborate, the handles decorated with leather or beadwork.

Best of all, but rarely obtainable because of the need to conserve endangered species, is an eagle-feather fan. Native North Americans believe that the prayers and thoughts contained in the smoke are carried to the Creator on the wings of eagles, who fly closest to the Sun.

Birds and their associations

Cockerel: Protection
Crane: Longevity and health
Crow: Change
Dove or pigeon: Reconciliation and love
Duck: Prosperity
Eagle: Nobility and vision
Falcon or kestrel: Focus
Goose: Domestic happiness
Hawk: Enlightenment
Ibis: Wisdom
Ostrich: Justice
Owl: Learning
Peacock: Lasting happiness
Pelican: Nurturing powers
Raven: Hidden potential
Seagull: Wide horizons
Stork: Fertility
Swan: Creativity and magic
Turkey: Abundance and altruism

Smudge books

It is very useful to keep a book in which you note the differences between herbs that burn well and those that are better smouldered on charcoal. You can also list any herbs that you find effective and the purpose for which you used them, for example healing. Note the combinations and proportions you used, too.

Record which herbs are more effective as smudge sticks and those that are better burned in a bowl.

It is so easy to forget, over even just a few months, as you are absorbing so much knowledge.

You can also write down any special rituals you carry out, either alone or as part of a group. These may be on the new Moon or as a rite of passage, perhaps a birth or marriage, or they may be the results of healing work, divination or meditation. Your smudge book will be a working manual, but you might also like to copy it into a leather- or cloth-bound volume, perhaps with pressed flowers or herbs from the sample you collected for smudging, and you can then hand it on to the next generation.

Storing your smudging equipment

I keep my smudge tools around my hearth, which is no longer used for open fires. However, for working in different places or out of doors, a carrying bag is necessary. What is more, if you have young children or share accommodation, you may want to keep your smudging tools separate from domestic life.

You can, if you like, follow the Native North American tradition and wrap sweetgrass braids, pieces of sagebrush or perhaps pine branches around your equipment and then fold everything into a large piece of soft leather or natural fabric, tied with natural cord. Leather and fabric drawstring bags are also ideal and widely available. You may find one with separate compartments for more delicate items, such as smudge sticks, or you can wrap these separately within the larger bag.

In your kitchen, or on shelves around your house or, like me, in your hearth, you can keep dark glass jars containing herbs you frequently use, for example, lavender heads or chamomile flowers. You can transfer smaller quantities for a ritual to a leather or fabric drawstring purse or small bags.

Your charcoal discs must also be kept dry – wrap them in foil or keep them in an airtight container.

Preparing for ritual

Every single aspect of a smudging ritual forms part of the ceremony, from crumbling herbs in a bowl to extinguishing your stick in sand or soil. Each stage can be an occasion for a silent or group prayer, asking blessings of your special deity form or of the benign forces of the universe.

Lighting a smudge stick

Smudge sticks are slow-burning herbs, tied together in a bundle. You can buy them ready-made or make your own (see pages 81–3).

Traditionally the end of the smudge stick or braid was lit from a communal fire, used for cooking and warmth as well as being the focus of the home. The hearth, it was believed, was where the ancestors as well as the living gathered – a belief that survives today in many lands. However, in practice, a candle or taper is the most practical and safest method of lighting a smudge stick.

Take your smudge stick to a candle and hold it momentarily in the flame so that you do not drip wax on to it. If possible, use a natural beeswax candle or one dyed naturally in green or brown, the colours of the Earth Mother. Alternatively, very long cook's matches are ideal. Light it in one or two places in the centre and when the flame dies down blow very gently upwards until the tip is glowing. As you do so, silently ask for blessings, and perhaps any particular needs of others and the land – and do not forget yourself.

If the flame looks too fierce on lighting, you can gently blow it out, as you would a candle.

If the stick looks as if it is going out during the ritual, blow on it gently upwards, using this breath for silent prayer. Sometimes a stick may look as if it is not burning when in fact it is smouldering inside. As I said earlier, you can make the re-lighting part of the ritual and add words such as:

Burn bright and true that the wishes may rise and blessings fall.

The technicalities of smudging become totally automatic after you have smudged a few times. It is a good idea to devote a number of sessions to getting to know your tools. Practise lighting, moving with the burning smudge, re-lighting and extinguishing (see the end of the chapter for one very basic ritual).

When you have finished smudging, gently extinguish the stick, giving thanks to the Earth and to the herbs. Wait till your stick is cool and scrape or cut off the burned herbs very gently; they will usually come away easily. You can re-use your stick many times and when it begins to fall apart, you can burn the remaining herbs in a bowl.

Lighting herbs in a bowl

Put sand or soil in the bottom of your dish, asking silently for blessings from the Earth Mother. Pile leaves in the centre so that no more than a third of the dish is covered, with leaves close together, one on top of the other. When you intend to burn an unfamiliar herb or flower in a ritual, test it first with just one or two leaves to see how it behaves.

Use tapers lit from a central candle or use very long cook's matches and light two or three large herbs in the centre. Make sure the flames are quite deep – don't just ignite the surface. Once the leaves have started to burn, you will need to blow out the flame almost at once, but then gently blow or fan the glowing herbs to get a stream of smoke going. The fanning can be made a regular part of the ritual: if you are working in a group it can be carried out as individuals speak; if you are alone, fan between the stages of your ritual.

Once ignited, bowls tend to be very good-tempered and burn more steadily than smudge sticks but, if you are moving the bowl, make sure that the handle or lip does remain cool or otherwise conduct your ritual round the bowl.

Like smudge sticks, bowls of herbs will eventually go out on their own, but should you need to extinguish them you can sprinkle sand or soil on the burning herbs or cover the dish with a heatproof lid. Some traditionalists believe water should not be used to extinguish sacred fire. My own feeling is that using water is messy and not generally recommended except, of course, in an emergency. Water should never be used to extinguish wax as it would cause a flare-up.

Cleansing your magical artefacts

After a ritual, once the bowl and any other implements are cool, they should be washed out and left to dry naturally, if possible in sunlight.

Bury any burned herbs and crumble your used smudge stick, or dispose of them in a bio-degradable brown paper bag.

If a ritual was for a special purpose or involved driving away negativity, you may wish to cleanse your artefacts psychically once you have washed them. You can also adapt this method for any cleansing equipment you buy that once belonged to someone else, or to remove the vibes of the person who packed them (see below).

Cleansing with sacred water

Cleansing can be carried out with sacred water. To make this, leave a bowl of water in the moonlight on the night of the full Moon, so that it turns silver. Keep a supply of sacred water in dark glass bottles for cleansing work. If you need or prefer to make your water at a different time of the month, boil nine tiny clear crystal quartz in two litres (about four pints) of water. (Nine is the number of perfection in many cultures.) Allow the water to cool and this time keep it in clear glass bottles so sunlight can filter in. This is an ancient Celtic method.

Sacred water is also restorative – sip it or add it to your bath to benefit from its health-giving properties.

To cleanse smudging equipment, sprinkle the artefacts with nine drops of sacred water that was collected under the full Moon, or rainwater that has not touched the ground. If you live in an area of acid rain, add nine drops of your favourite flower or tree essence (see Useful Addresses, pages 186–7).

Cleansing with salt

To cleanse a partly used smudge stick, surround it with a circle of salt and sprinkle the circle with the sacred water rather than applying water to the stick.

Restoring energies

After a ritual, you can restore energies to your smudging equipment by using a pendulum. Pendulums are used for all kinds of ritual and magic; the hypnotist's watch swinging on its chain is a good example. They can be made from almost anything – one of the most effective I ever saw was a plumb bob on an old curtain cord. You can buy a crystal, metal or wooden pendulum or use a favourite charm or crystal on a chain. I have seen expert dowsers improvise with a key on a piece of string. However, for ritual work, a crystal hung on a thread or chain is the most popular type.

To cleanse and restore energies to an item of smudging equipment, hold a clear crystal pendulum over it and make nine anti-clockwise circles. Plunge the pendulum in cold running water to cleanse it, shake it dry and then circle it nine times clockwise over the tools to restore energies. The clockwise movement of a pendulum always signifies positive energies.

You may need to repeat this several times if an artefact seems lifeless or you have carried out a banishing ritual.

A blessing ritual using a smudge stick

This ritual is good for those occasions when you have an important day ahead of you, or an arduous journey to undertake. If it is fine, go out of doors and visualise a circle of light surrounding you. If not, work indoors so there is space all around you.

Arrangements for the ritual

Have your bowl of earth or sand ready in advance in the centre of the circle and your beeswax candle on a plinth or a table on a fireproof tray. (Remember, never try to extinguish burning wax with water.)

If possible, carry out the ritual as dawn is breaking.

* Facing East, light a sage smudge stick. When the flame has burned down, blow gently upwards nine times. Take a pause between each so the stick does not glow too fiercely.
* With each breath, silently ask a separate blessing, linked with the endeavour on which the ritual is focused.
* When your smudge is burning, again facing East, make nine clockwise circles of smoke around you, saying:

One, bless this new day and the promises it brings.
Two, bless the birds that soar and sing that anything is possible.
Three, bless the insects who teach perseverance and that the greatest endeavour may grow from the smallest beginnings.

Four, bless the trees who join Earth to Sky,
body with spirit and heart to mind.
Five, bless these sacred herbs that willingly offer their strengths to
increase my own, their purity to cleanse my life of doubt and fear and
their courage to uplift me on my journey.
Six, bless the flame of this stick that illumines, inspires
and brings light out of darkness, optimism and enthusiasm
for what may not be expected.
Seven, bless the wise ancestors whose own journeys and endeavours
brought me to this place at this time, and whose inner counsel
continues to guide me.
Eight, bless my friends and family who help and support me, offering
the sure foundations from which I venture, and to which I will return
welcomed equally in triumph or disaster.
Nine, bless the source of light and life and goodness that courses
through me as through all creation and unites us
in the Sacred Hoop of existence.
Blessings be.

* Stand in silence, holding your smudge stick, and allow the smoke in its own way to enfold you in protection.
* Finally offer your stick in silence to the six directions and then gently extinguish it in the central bowl of sand, lifting it out and shaking off any excess, saying:

Burn bright within me sacred fire that will never be extinguished so
long as the world endures.

You can adapt this ritual to any purpose, making the nine smoke circles around you. For example, if you need an urgent injection of money, as you make the circles you could chant:

Grandmother Spider bring to me, wealth and prosperity.

* Chant faster and faster and visualise golden coins falling from the sky and golden wheat or corn springing up around your feet.

This ritual rarely fails for me in offering inspiration (although not always an instant cheque for some long-forgotten foreign royalties that have been gathering dust in my publisher's office).

Chapter 3
Creating Ritual

The Medicine Wheel

The Medicine Wheel is the area of sacred space central to Native North American spirituality. 'Medicine' in this case means power or energy and represents the life force flowing through all creation in the sacred circle of existence. Each of the quadrants of the circle is associated with particular colours, animals, crystals and herbs. There are almost 500 different forms of Medicine or Power Wheels in North America alone, so there is great variation in the associations (on pages 148–51 you will find a six-herb ritual that incorporates these energies). Some of the Native North American Medicine Wheels were 30 metres (90 feet) in diameter but research suggests that many were much smaller and placed around ceremonial tepees, to be used not only by shamans but also by anyone seeking a spiritual path.

The image of a magic circle is also used in western ceremonial and ritual magic – the great stone circles of Europe and Scandinavia were created from about 3500 BC and were used for ceremonies on the solstices and the equinoxes.

Over the years, in the industrialised West, there has arisen a division between secular and spiritual life, but increasingly people are recognising that, by restoring unity of mind, body, spirit and different aspects of our worlds, we can avoid fragmentation and the discontent and unhappiness it brings.

Even though you may use your smudging in an entirely different world from that of Native North America, the Medicine Wheel is a very powerful way of marking sacred space and making the connection through ritual between humans, nature and the world of Spirit.

Symbolism of the Medicine Wheel

The basic form of the Medicine Wheel is a cross in a circle. The north–south axis represents the connection between Heaven and Earth and the east–west division represents the path of human life within time and history. The connections between all existence from the weather to the tiniest insect are central to Native North American wisdom. This is how they were described by Black Elk, the Sioux shaman:

In the old days when we were a strong and happy people, all our power came from the Sacred Hoop of the nation and so long as the Hoop was unbroken, the people flourished. The flowering tree was the living centre of the Hoop and the circle of the four quarters nourished it. The East gave peace and light, the South gave warmth; in the West thunder beings gave rain, and the North with its cold and mighty wind gave strength and endurance.

The significance of the four cardinal directions corresponds very closely with the westernised elemental system. In both the western magical system, which uses a magic circle, and the Native American Medicine Wheel, the directions of North, East, South and West are important marker points symbolically, and correspond to different seasons and times of day that are the same in both systems. The Medicine Wheel tends to focus on the East, the direction of the rising

Sun, as the first direction to be faced, and this also corresponds with some forms of westernised magic.

In this book, I do not attempt to recreate the secret, sacred and sometimes sadly forgotten ceremonies of the indigenous peoples of North America. But whatever our lifestyle or culture, the tradition can strengthen or restore our connections with the natural world and the world of Spirit.

The four cardinal directions are watched over by guardians, sometimes addressed as the Grandfathers or Grandmothers.

However, the other two directions are equally important and form the invisible axis that passes through the centre of the Wheel, from the male World Tree to the female circle. Below is Mother Earth, and above is Father Sky. Increasingly, I am recognising that these fifth and sixth directions are important in all forms of magic.

Around the Wheel are set totem animals, one for each birth month. For the purposes of this book, I have concentrated on the four main animal and bird rulers of the cardinal directions and seasons, plus the animals that correspond to the Sky and the Earth, who sit respectively at the top and bottom of the central invisible tree or totem pole. The totems vary according to each nation's mythology and I have chosen those that are common to a number of systems.

The animals of the Wheel

The totem animals that rule the four quarters and the seasons are in themselves symbols of the specific powers and wisdom they possess. You can visualise them as you work, or you may wish to carve them from wood or create clay representations or figures from plaster moulds to stand at the four main direction points. This works particularly well in a garden circle, where you could set smaller statues of the creatures on small logs or tables or even obtain the stone kind used as garden ornaments and paint them in brilliant colours. However, if they are small enough they can be used indoors.

You could paint or carve the Sky and Earth totems on a mini totem pole to stand in the middle of the circle, or place the Sky totem on top of a post or tall tree stump and the Earth animal at the foot. If you are very ingenious, you can adapt a tall central table or narrow free-standing display shelf so it will also hold your working smudge tools. Alternatively, you can place any Sky symbol to the left of the Earth symbol in the centre of the circle. Again, if space is a problem, you can simply visualise them.

The Hawk

The Hawk rules the East, spring and the dawn.

He soars through the air, like the Eagle that rules the Sky direction. He is a creature who flies close to the Sun. He represents the desire to explore, to search for truth rather than focusing on personal gain. Sometimes, like the Eagle, he is associated with the legendary Thunder Bird, the rain-bringer, whose flashing eyes are lightning and flapping wings bring thunder, and also with the power of the Sun.

The Hawk was one of the creatures that helped to create the world after the Flood. He hunts for need, killing for food not pleasure, and his vision is acute, focused and perfectly honed upon his target.

Be single-minded and pursue what is of worth: this is the Hawk's message.

The Stag

The Stag rules the South, the summer and noon.

He is the mighty hunter, the symbol of potency, who must fight to win and maintain supremacy. He exalts in and maximises his potency and vitality, knowing it will not last forever. In many of the ancient religions, the Horned God, or supreme being, was Lord of the Wild who would be killed and replaced by his son/successor.

Make the most of every opportunity and golden moment: this is the message of the Stag.

The Salmon

The Salmon rules the West, autumn and the dusk.

She is the tribal Mother of Fish and totem of all life returning to source. Because the Salmon will swim hundreds of miles to return to her place of birth, leaping high waterfalls to spawn her young, she has come to represent the essential unchanging self in a rapidly moving world. Salmon may die after breeding but they have fulfilled their destiny and ensured the continuation of life.

The Salmon can assure you of who you really are. We all have a core self, which, no matter how far we travel or whatever we achieve, will remain permanent despite triumph or misfortune.

Return to the source of wisdom and be true to yourself: this is the message of the Salmon.

The Bear

The Bear rules the North, winter and midnight.

He represents primal strength, protection and noble purpose and was regarded as an ancestor by some tribes and as a bridge between the animal, human and spirit kingdoms.

Because bears hibernate in caves (the womb of the supreme female being) and the female bear nurtures her young for many years, they possess strong maternal qualities expressed as fierceness, especially in protecting their young. Bears are also associated with healing because it is believed that they are able to identify the right herbs to cure specific illnesses or wounds.

Be self-sufficient, not selfish: this is the message of the Bear.

The Eagle

The Eagle rules the Sky and is positioned above the centre of the Wheel.

He is tribal chief of all birds and soars high in the sky, yet sees everything below. He is, like the Hawk, connected with the Thunder Bird.

In Native North American lore, the feathers of the eagle carry the prayers of the people to the Father Sun. It was said that the eagle could fly closer than any creature to the Sun and not be burned; he could also look into the noonday Sun without flinching and not be blinded. Because of his association with the Sky Fathers in many cultures, he is a totem that represents limitless potential, broad vision and idealism. Eagle feathers are a symbol of healing wisdom.

Aim high and do not sacrifice your principles: this is the Eagle's message.

The Buffalo

The Buffalo rules the Earth, growth and nourishment, womb and tomb.

She is the bringer of abundance.

She is positioned at the foot of the invisible axis, in the centre of the Medicine Wheel. However, in a number of Native North American rituals, for example the Sun Dance held around the summer solstice or at the beginning of August, a buffalo skull would be placed on top of the central post.

To the Native North American Indian nations, the buffalo was the source of everything needed for survival, flesh for food, bones for cooking implements, weapons and tools, skin for clothes and covering the tepees and sinews for sewing thread.

According to the legend of White Buffalo Calf Woman, she not only brought knowledge of healing and agriculture to the Lakota nations, but promised that she would return to lead the people into the revival of their spirituality after the sufferings that would come. In reality, even though the buffalo herds were almost wiped out by the nineteenth-century settlers, a white buffalo calf born recently in Wisconsin has become a symbol of hope to all the Native North American nations.

Give freely of yourself and your gifts and your own needs will be provided: this is the message of the Buffalo.

Setting up a Medicine Wheel

You can make your own Medicine Wheel to be used as a central focus for your rituals.

Making a temporary Medicine Wheel

Create a simple circle of stones, branches, crystals, rushes, branches or chalk, if possible out of doors. You can also draw one in the earth with a stick or in sand on a beach and allow the tide to carry the magical energies on the waves after the ritual.

Divide the circle into four segments, again using stones or chalk, so the circle is bisected from North to South and East to West.

Making a permanent Medicine Wheel

You may wish to make a more permanent Medicine Wheel for your personal or group smudging work in your garden or a spare room, perhaps painted on the bare floor and covered over with a rug when not in use.

Paint each arm in the colours suggested below for the four directions or use other colour correspondences given in this section. In each of the four segments, scatter either fresh sage or rosemary (a herb of love) or newly mown grass cuttings. Alternatively, use some of the herbs listed below.

Place four candles or outdoor garden flares in the colours of the four cardinal directions; these vary according to the tradition you follow. For example, the Oglala Sioux associate black with the West, white with the North, red with the East and yellow with the South. However, in the western magical tradition, North is green or brown, the East yellow, the South red or orange and the West blue.

If you want to have candles in the centre, use gold for Father Sky on the left and silver or natural, undyed beeswax for Mother Earth on the right.

You can also set crystals at the four marker points: citrine or clear crystal quartz to the East, carnelian or amber to the South, jade or aventurine to the West and obsidian or bloodstone to the North. In the centre set turquoise or dyed blue howzite for the Sky and fossilised wood or banded agate for the Earth.

Herbs for your Medicine Wheel

According to Native North American tradition, particular herbs are associated with each of the six directions of the Medicine Wheel.

East: Lavender, mint and lemongrass
South: Bay, chamomile and rosemary
West: Cedar, rose petals or thyme
North: Cypress, pine or mugwort
Father Sky (upwards): Desert sage
Mother Earth (downwards): Sweetgrass or grey sage

You can place tiny dishes of these in each of the quadrants with your Sky and Earth in the centre to the left and right. On pages 148–51 I describe a ritual for burning each of these.

A Medicine Wheel ritual for meditation

Smudging with a Medicine Wheel is a way of integrating the powers of the six directions, as manifest in their power animals. Some people burn different herbs for each direction, but in practice a single smudge stick or bowl offered with chants or prayers in each of the different directions in turn is an excellent way of awakening psychic senses, and this can form a ritual in itself. Sage is the herb most often chosen for this.

Arrangements for the ritual

Rather than creating an actual Medicine Wheel, you can, if you wish, visualise one. It may be set high on a plateau in the mountains, on a shore, in the desert or in a clearing in a forest with the power animals and birds arranged around the rim and the Wheel itself illuminated by the rising Sun.

Smudging and incense burning

You can also work within a circle of coloured candles if you wish (see page 62 for the colours of each segment). Set a candle in the centre, ready to light your taper. You can use a bowl of herbs or a smudge stick, whichever you prefer.

* Stand in the centre of your real or visualised Medicine Wheel, facing East. See ahead of you the Hawk sitting at the eastern compass point.
* Light a taper from the central candle, then light your herbs and blow or fan gently until they are glowing; as you do so, visualise the creatures sitting still around you, vigilant and protective.
* When you have a single steady stream of smoke, go to the eastern edge of the circle. Make clockwise circles of smoke above the head of the Hawk, saying:

Hawk of the East, fly true. I take into my centre your focus, your power to rise above the mundane and to live by your own efforts, seeking the favours of none.

* Visualise the Hawk rising.
* Carry the glowing herbs back into the centre. Circle your heart and then smudge a clockwise spiral of smoke from your crown, down the front of your body and then up your back, ending where you began, saying:

With thanks I take into myself the power of the Hawk and the clarity of the East.

* Turn and move to the South, visualising a mighty Stag, motionless in the thicket. Over him, smudge a rising clockwise circle of smoke, saying:

Stag of the South, shining golden as the Sun, I take into my centre your swiftness, courage and ability to confront life without turning aside or running in terror from the foe.

* Visualise the Stag turning and proudly galloping into the forest and carry your bowl or smudge stick back to the centre of the circle.
* Again lightly smudge yourself, beginning with your heart, then your crown, saying:

With thanks I take into myself the power of the Stag and the inspiration of the South.

* Turn and move to the West. At the compass point, visualise a Salmon leaping high from a waterspout. Walk towards the Salmon and swirl your smudge stick or fan the herbs upwards and clockwise, saying:

Salmon of the West, leaping high, I take into my centre your ceaseless journeying, your perseverance, your unerring instinct to find your home and above all your willingness to embrace your destiny.

* Visualise the Salmon leaping into a deep pool and carry the herbs back into the centre.
* Again smudge yourself lightly, beginning with the heart, saying:

With thanks I take in the power of the salmon and the fertility of the West.

* Turn and move next to the North, seeing the Bear standing near her den. Move gently, quietly reassuring her you mean no harm, and smudge a circle over her. Say:

Bear of the North, I take into my centre your nurturing and protection of all who are vulnerable, your strength, your healing wisdom and your ability to adapt to any season or stage of life.

✳ Visualise the Bear going into her den. Carry the herbs to the centre of the circle and, still facing the North, lightly smudge yourself, again beginning with your heart, saying:

With thanks I take into myself the wisdom of the Bear and the protection of the North.

✳ Now standing in the centre, see the Eagle soaring above you and raise your smudge stick or bowl so the smoke curls upwards, saying:

I give thanks, Eagle Father, and ask that your vision and limitless potential may enter and inspire my centre of being.

✳ In silence, smudge yourself lightly, this time spiralling from the top to the bottom of your body.

✳ Finally, standing in the centre, press down on to the Earth with your feet and hear the thunder of the hooves of the Buffalo. Swirl the smoke downwards to the ground saying:

I give thanks, Mother Buffalo, and ask that your abundance and generosity may enter and inspire my centre of being.

✳ Smudge yourself lightly, from the feet upwards, seeing the smoke linking the Buffalo and Eagle in a single axis.

✳ Sit quietly in the centre on a blanket and allow the smudge herbs to burn through, letting visions of the animals and their messages for you come and go.

If you are in a hurry, you can simply acknowledge the six directions with a curl of smoke as you stand in the centre of your actual or visualised Wheel. Ask the blessings of each animal as you face its direction.

Like the Native North Americans, who followed the migration of the buffalo and built a new Medicine Wheel each time the tribe moved, you can make an impromptu Wheel wherever you are. It may be made of sticks or stones or simply visualised in your mind's eye. Any outdoor place will do, for example by running water or near an ancient site (many are still entirely open to the public, especially in remoter places). In time, you may dream of your animals and hear them speak words of wisdom to you as you face the different directions. Each person uses his or her Medicine Wheel in a unique way.

Times of the day for smudging

Dawn: This is a magical time especially for purification ceremonies, for changing luck and clearing away stagnant energies.

Noon: Noon offers full energy for empowerment ceremonies, for charging magical tools and possessions, for cleansing the home and workspace and for healing rituals to attract strength and health.

Dusk: This is the time for removing pain and banishing old sorrows, for magical rituals of all kinds, and for divination.

Midnight: Midnight is the best time for welcoming the wise ancestors, for protective rituals to banish fear and psychic or psychological attacks, and for peace.

The cycles of the Moon

The Moon cycle can be divided into the waxing phase from the new Moon to the full Moon for all matters of increase, and from the full Moon to the end of the cycle for purification. If both aspects are involved in your ceremony, choose the one that is predominant at that time. The day of the full Moon and one day on either side of it make up a period of maximum power which is also good for great change and transformation. So if your need is urgent or great or you are smudging for a life change or for a reversal of a particular situation, this is the time.

You can if you wish blend your Moon and Sun energies for maximum effect. So, for example, noon on the day of the full Moon is most potent of all. Use a good diary with the rising and setting times of the Moon and Sun (remember to allow for time zone differences). Time your rituals so you can invoke and harmonise the powers of both the Sun and the Moon when both are in the sky at the same time. You will notice that the times vary from month to month because of the irregularity of the Moon's orbit.

For example, on 3 November 2000, the fifth day after the new Moon, the waxing Moon rose at 13.26 and set at 21.55 (I am using Greenwich Mean Time). The Sun on the same day rose at 06.57 and set at 16.29. Since it was clear day where I lived, I used the waxing Moon and the solar energies together and after dusk the Moon was visible in the sky for five hours.

Of course, you can smudge at any time during any phase of the Moon if you have a specific need. Human emotion, especially when directed altruistically, is the most powerful magical energy of all.

Chapter 4
Choosing and Using Herbs for Smudging

Smudging is, in essence, a folk magic and there is a vast amount of herb lore, based on the indigenous plants of areas throughout the world. As a result, a very wide variety of herbs is used for smudging. At one time people even smudged with unprocessed tobacco but, in view of the almost universal health problems caused by cigarettes, this is rarely used although the Native North American Indians still regard it as a sacred gift brought to the home by visitors.

The three herbs most commonly used for smudging are, as I said earlier, cedar, sage and sweetgrass. Juniper, which is similar to cedar, and pine are also particularly common as they grow wild in many parts of the world. Just outside my own caravan are pine trees that frequently shed huge pieces of brush that are excellent for smudging as well as for putting outside the door in the muddy months both as a carpet and for mystical protection.

You can experiment with a variety of herbs. I have given a full list of 65 in Chapter 11, and on page 182 in the Further Reading section I have also suggested books that describe the healing and magical properties of other herbs.

Choosing herbs for smudging

Later in this chapter, I give a list of the most common smudging herbs. I have included the three core Native North American smudge herbs, though it should be remembered that these have far greater sacred significance than the others.

Your choice of herbs for smudging will be governed by practical as well as personal considerations.

On the practical side, you will find that some varieties of common herbs are better than others for different kinds of smudging – experiment with small quantities and note your results in your smudge book. When trying out herbs you have not burned before, always test them by lighting a few crushed dried herbs – or herbs strands if you intend to make smudge sticks from them – in a shallow dish and see how they burn. Some burn too fiercely, so that you cannot obtain a steady stream of smoke; some will not burn at all; and some simply smell awful. If this is the case, try smouldering them on charcoal (see pages 37–8 for instructions on lighting) and you will find that your lavender or chamomile becomes wonderfully fragrant. Remember to note your findings for future reference.

Cost may also be an important consideration. Dried herbs specially prepared for smudging can be quite expensive. I get my chamomile, lavender and bay leaves from a very old-fashioned grocer's in my local market town at a fraction of the price I would pay for commercially packed 'smudge' herbs. Look out for bargain buys, perhaps in large quantities. In a French supermarket I found packs of large pieces of dried thyme and I was able to burn these directly in a bowl.

Also note that many of the commercial sticks that contain herbs such as lavender enclose them in bulkier herbs such as white sage.

One useful tip I have discovered is to keep any leaves that come away when I scrape away the burned part of a sage smudge stick; these shavings, placed in a bowl, are excellent for getting more reluctant herbs started.

On page 79 I describe ways of drying your own herbs if you want to carry the whole process through from start to finish – this is the cheapest option of all.

I mentioned above that, in addition to practicalities, your choice of herbs might well be governed by personal considerations. By this I meant that you will probably want to choose the herbs whose properties you like – such as their smell. Once again, experimentation is the key: some plants do smell quite different when burned, and you may prefer ready-prepared incenses where the fragrance of the burned stick, cone or granules are the same as the unburned product.

Raid your culinary herb or spice rack or use dried flowers, leaves, etc., and drop a small amount of each on burning charcoal to see which you like. Note down any effective combinations. Notice also how you feel – elated, thoughtful, or peaceful – as people do react quite differently to fragrances.

You will also want to choose herbs that will have a positive effect on your life. Here I have listed common herbs for smudging, together with their most powerful properties.

Bay: For health and fidelity

Bay leaf is best burned on charcoal to release the fragrance. However, you can also use the greenery in a smudge stick as its leaves are quite solid, but use only a small proportion and mix it with slower-burning herbs, such as sage or cedar, as it burns too fiercely alone.

It will prevent bad dreams and drive away bad luck, especially when burned on charcoal with mugwort. Bay will bring good health and encourage trust and faithfulness in relationships. It offers psychic protection and healing of sorrow, purifying all forms of pollution and negativity, and is therefore good for smudging rites for healing the planet or a specific area.

Cedar: For cleansing and protection

Cedar is the one of the trilogy of Native North American sacred herbs. It may be burned either as a smudge stick or in a bowl.

It is a herb of purification, protection and healing and is a good herb for the home, where it may be used to protect tools and special artefacts you may have (see pages 24–5).

Chamomile: For gentleness and children

Chamomile is excellent burned either alone on charcoal or with lavender heads. Occasionally it is found enclosed within sturdier smudge herbs in a stick.

It is a good herb for deflecting anger or hostility and for protecting children. It also attracts abundance and prosperity. It is good for meditation and for attracting new love, family happiness and the growth of trust after betrayal and loss. Chamomile is also protective, and deters those who would do harm.

Juniper: For cleansing

Juniper berries are traditionally dried, crushed and burned as part of a cleansing rite, especially at New Year in Scotland. Berries are best burned on charcoal but you can also make smudge sticks with juniper leaf sprigs. Juniper wood spits a great deal when lit, so proceed carefully. The greenery is sometimes substituted for cedar in smudge bundles or bowls with sage and sweetgrass as this is a very potent mix for cleansing a negative atmosphere in the home or around your person.

Juniper is protective against accidents, negative psychic forces, violence and sickness. It also increases psychic awareness when used in a smudge stick.

Lavender: For peace and reconciliation

Lavender works especially well in the middle of bulkier herbs in a smudge stick as it is too flimsy alone. You can burn the dried flower heads separately on charcoal.

Alone or mixed with other healing herbs, lavender will create a peaceful atmosphere. It also attracts loving energies and spirits and is good for emotional cleansing. It is used for sending wishes into the cosmos.

Lavender combined with rosemary encourages positive thoughts and an ability to see possibilities and to persevere even in the most unpromising situations or relationships. A combination of lavender and thyme will restore stability in uncertain or challenging times and help you establish priorities.

Like cedar, lavender is a harmoniser, both in relation to other people and within the different aspects of the self.

Mint: For the expansion of horizons and prosperity

Mint burns best alone on charcoal to release the fragrance, but can be put in the centre of broad-leaved smudge sticks. I find it is both uplifting and cleansing and is particularly good when used in combination with sage or cedar.

It is a healing and purifying herb, especially good for domestic protection and at home or in sickrooms to drive away all negativity and illness. It also attracts money and travel opportunities.

Mugwort: For psychic awareness and prophetic dreams

Mugwort is best combined with sage in the centre of smudge sticks but can also be burned alone, either as a smudge stick if the leaves are firm or separately in a bowl. You may need charcoal.

Mugwort is used for healing, divination and to stimulate dreams and visions. It can be burned during rituals or before sleeping. However, as some people find it slightly mind-altering, you should avoid using it before driving. It is very protective and banishes psychic and psychological attacks.

Orris root: For psychic ability and protection

Orris root may be used with the leaves as the inner part of a smudge stick. Alternatively, you can burn it in a bowl but you may need charcoal to get it going.

Combined with celery seeds, orris increases psychic gifts and concentration, and when used with sage it protects against physical, psychological and psychic malevolence. From the Florentine iris, the powdered root smells like violets.

Pine, fir and spruce: For purification

All three of these evergreens are burned for their purifying and cleansing effect. You can burn the needles in a bowl or make them into smudge sticks. Sometimes pine is combined in smudge sticks with other herbs, especially juniper, as it will enhance their effects. Piñon pine is especially resinous and needs to be burned on charcoal.

When burned before divination, pine ensures that a reading will be accurate, and in the everyday world it can also offer the courage to continue on a difficult path or to stand apart from the crowd when a matter of integrity is at stake.

Very protective, pine returns negativity to the sender and it is especially potent if it is gathered at midsummer.

Rose: For love and healing

You can burn rose petals on charcoal to release the fragrance. In my opinion, rose is not good for smudge sticks, though you can insert buds, leaves and stems stripped of thorns in the centre of a smudge stick.

Rose is used in love rituals of all kind and it is excellent for driving away fears and anxiety and for relieving old sorrows.

Rosemary: For clarity and healing

Rosemary is often included in commercial smudge sticks, especially those directed towards arousing love, an important secondary property. With all fine-leaved herbs it is important to make sure you use leafy sprigs with as little twiggy stem as possible. I have also burned rosemary alone as a smudge stick, but you do need to make the smudge sticks thick and pack them very tightly to stop them falling apart on lighting. It can also be burned in a bowl, and the powdered herbs with parsley, sage and thyme can be used on charcoal before divination.

Smudging with rosemary improves memory, focuses thoughts and increases energy levels. It will help to heal destructive or confrontational relationships, as well as protecting against illness. It is known as the herb of remembrance, especially of love, and can bring about reconciliation.

Sage: For transformation and empowerment

Another of the Native North American sacred herbs, white or desert sage is associated with Grandfather Sun and Father Sky, and grey sage with the Mother Goddess (see pages 23–4). Both can be burned as sticks or loose in a bowl. Culinary sage can also be burned but is best on charcoal, though it will burn as a stick.

All sages are cleansing and empowering and so are excellent all-purpose herbs for absolutely any ritual.

Sweetgrass: For positive energies, gentleness and healing

The last of the Native North American sacred herbs, sweetgrass is a herb of the Mother Goddess. Burn it as braids, either held in the hand or in a bowl.

Sweetgrass brings gentle healing and attracts abundance in all aspects of life (see pages 25–7).

Thyme: For prophecy and mental acuity

Another divinatory herb, thyme can be added to smudge sticks or used alone if packed tightly or burned in a bowl. For these purposes, use the broad-leaved kind.

An aid to memory, thyme is a health-bringer and can aid recall of the past and allow glimpses into the future. It also gives courage and strength. Thyme drives away dark dreams and replaces them with good ones. Excellent also for all divination work as thyme is said to increase prophetic powers.

Yarrow: For fidelity and psychic awareness

Firm yarrow sprigs can be made into smudge sticks and yarrow may also be burned in a bowl or combined with other herbs in a stick.

Yarrow was traditionally burned for an enduring relationship over many years, at weddings and the renewal of vows. It is also burned during divination and meditation.

Yerba santa: For increasing beauty in people and places, and for purification

Yerba santa can be burned in a bowl or added to sage smudge sticks.

When burned with rosemary or lavender in a bowl on charcoal, the herb will attract love and link you with the natural world and the instinctive wisdom of the ancestors. It tends to be used as an ecological healer, protecting boundaries of places, including homes. Burn it also for courage and increased psychic awareness.

Growing herbs

If you do not have a garden, you can plant window boxes of herbs or keep them in your home. The kitchen can be too hot, so use a sheltered hallway or a corner of the living room where natural light falls. A conservatory or balcony is ideal. If you have a garden and can put aside a small area for a herb plot, bury a small clear quartz crystal, green jasper or moss agate in each corner of the plot.

If any herb looks as if it is going to wilt, place a piece of jade or moss agate in water for 24 hours and then use this to water the plant.

If you have individual pots of herbs, plant a tiny quartz crystal in each (you can buy boxes of tiny mixed crystals). This will energise the soil and protect your plants from predatory insects.

Basil is a natural insect repellent, so include this in any plot if possible.

Harvesting your herbs

As a general rule, leaves should be gathered before the buds and blooms appear, and flowers taken before fruits and seeds appear. Those parts of the plant above ground should be harvested in the morning, before the heat of the Sun has a chance to wilt them, if possible while the dew is still around.

Bark and roots are best taken in early spring or autumn. If bark is needed, strip it from small patches or particular branches to avoid damaging the whole tree or plant. Roots should be carefully washed, scraped, and chopped into small pieces so they will be dry throughout.

Drying herbs

Drying herbs is very easy, and you will save a great deal of money if you grow and dry your own for use in smudge sticks and bowls.

If you are using an entire plant, hang it upside-down in a warm, dry area or at a north-facing window to dry. Make sure that the herbs are completely dry before storing them. It will take from two to three weeks.

Spread individual sprigs or flower heads for burning in a bowl in a warm, dry place on muslin-covered racks. Drying these takes less time than the whole plant, generally from two to ten days, but check them regularly. They should not be allowed to go brown.

You may have read that you can dry herbs in the oven or even in the microwave, but these are not suitable for smudging as they lose much of their fragrance and texture and tend to crumble.

Storing dried herbs

Make sure your herbs are completely dry before packing them for storage.

Leaves and blossoms can be stored either whole or crushed. Place the herbs in airtight containers, preferably of coloured glass to keep out light rather than plastic, which can taint them. Keep the containers in a dry, cool area away from light. If stored correctly, they will last for up to a year.

Lunar herb gardening

Because of their magical associations, the planting, care and cutting of herbs, even more than other plants, have been governed by the phases of the Moon. This practice has come to be known as lunar gardening. Research on both sides of the Atlantic and in the Antipodes has suggested that the old beliefs are supported by botanical studies as well as by the experiences of gardeners worldwide.

Planting on the waxing Moon

The majority of herbs should be planted during the waxing phase of the Moon. This is the 14 days from the new to the full Moon. Herbs planted during this period have been shown to prosper more than those grown during the waning half of the lunar month (the 14 days from the full Moon to the end of the lunar month). The days closest to the appearance of the full Moon are best of all. Most newspapers and diaries have entries to tell you which phase the Moon is in.

Herb-planting months

Although herbs can be planted at any time of the year, except for the very cold times, the best periods are said to be during the sway of the Water signs of the zodiac in the waxing period of the Moon. The Water signs are Cancer (22 June–22 July), Pisces (19 February–20 March) and Scorpio (24 October–22 November).

There are exceptions: for example, sage should be planted during the week of the full Moon in the sign of Pisces, Scorpio or Cancer. Valerian, the soothing herb of body and mind similar to vervain (see page 179), should be planted during the waxing half of the month in either Gemini (22 May–21 June) or Virgo (24 August–22 September).

Times for cutting herbs

Pruning and cutting herbs for use are best done during the waning half of the lunar month. The best periods are said to be during Aquarius, Aries, Gemini, Leo and Virgo. The moment the Moon turns full is also sometimes favoured, as the plant is then believed to retain its full vitality.

Friday, because of its associations with the Crucifixion, is considered a bad day for planting or cutting herbs. Sunday has inherited from the Christian tradition the religious taboos of not working on the Sabbath. This applies of course to any other holy days, according to different faiths. In Ireland, the belief persists that herbs pulled on a Sunday lack flavour if eaten and their medicinal value is poor.

Making a smudge stick

Whether you grow your own herbs or buy them in pots or bundles, you can save money by making your own smudge sticks. This is remarkably easy with practice. The secret is to pack and entwine your herbs really tightly so that they will not fall apart when you light them.

Choose the twine you intend to use carefully. Avoid any synthetic ones and try to buy flame-retardant thread if possible. It should be strong but not thick. Before tying up your bundle of herbs, test it by burning a little in your flat dish. Does it flare up or smell foul? Horse tail is said to be the best, but is not easy to obtain. Experiment with undyed, natural twines and those made using vegetable colouring until you find one that works well for you.

You may wish to spend a special evening making your smudge sticks, either alone or with friends, beginning with picking the herbs. On pages 28–9 I described a ceremony of empowerment and this can be adapted your smudge stick making.

Pick a time of day when you can relax and enjoy your task. You can work out of doors in the early morning or indoors by the light of a beeswax candle as dusk approaches. Or perhaps you prefer to work out of doors in the warm afternoon sunshine, with the humming of bees and bird song around, visualising warm fields of fragrant herbs stretching endlessly like a green or golden sea. As you bind your herbs, be aware of the spirit of the plants, offering itself for your use, and give thanks silently, naming the purpose or person for whom the bundle is being made. Afterwards, you can plant a few seeds or clear some litter as a way of thanking Mother Earth for her bounty.

Use thick sprigs of the fresh herbs about 23–30 cm (9–12 in) long. Choose sprigs with plenty of greenery. The bunch for each stick should have about seven or eight sprigs in total.

Find a strong twig to use as a base around which you can twine the stems to give the bundle substance. You can use a central, very sturdy herb as an anchor, if you prefer. Taper the twig at one end so that the woody part you hold is slightly narrower. Broader smudge sticks tend to work better than narrow ones.

Hold the herbs tightly together and, starting from the stem end, bind them with thread in a criss-cross pattern. Knot them very tightly at 1 cm (½ in) intervals. The binding should reach between three-quarters and seven-eighths of the way up the smudge bundle. Finish off by making a loop of thread to hang the bundle up to dry.

If you want to add smaller or more slender herbs, such as lavender, chamomile or rose buds, use large, firm leaves on the outside to act as the container for the smaller herbs. First gather the smaller herbs into a bundle, then add the larger leaves as you begin to bind the stick.

Hang your smudge bundles upside-down to dry so that the air can circulate. Ensure the area you keep them in is not damp; it should be warm, but not exposed to direct sunlight.

Leave the bundles to dry for two to three weeks. They are ready for use as smudge sticks when they are dry but not brown.

Test your smudge stick by lighting it over a bowl – if it does fall apart, you have not wasted the effort and can burn the herbs in the bowl, adding wishes or blessings as you crumble the stick.

Chapter 5
Traditional Rituals in the Modern World

You can smudge at absolutely any time and in any place, and you can turn the simplest of actions into a short but meaningful ritual – even the act of lighting a cleansing incense stick such as pine in a room as people come home for the evening. Every time you spiral the smoke of a smudge stick around your body and over your head for cleansing or healing, you are creating a personal ceremony

In this section I have gathered together various traditional methods of smudging, and modified them slightly where necessary, to demonstrate how smudging can become a part of your everyday world as well as for special occasions.

Ultimately, smudging is a tool and there are many variations in its use both within and beyond the Native North American world. Like all good forms of spirituality, its methods are not set in stone. No guru, no matter how impeccable his or her pedigree (and some of the most egotistical I have met have their roots and tepees set firmly in Rotherham or Bournemouth earth), can state definitely what is right and what is wrong.

Whether you use incense or smudge sticks, or burn herbs in a bowl, what you feel and what you say are largely a private matter between you, the cosmos and Mother Earth. That relationship is as valid and can be just as close whether you live in the wild mountains or 20 storeys up in a tower block. You can use smudging for protection and empowerment in a remarkable number of ways (limited only by your own ingenuity), but it is always a blessing, bestowed on us by the herbs and so is a gift from Mother Nature. This makes it different from other less nature-centred rituals. Smudging is often less about asking for specifics (though of course you can when you have a need) than about receiving and giving thanks for blessings as part of the natural abundance that is shed daily.

Preparing yourself for ritual

Formal smudging, whether in a group or alone, marks a deliberate movement away from the everyday world, defining a special time and space. Preparation is an important and integral part of this demarcation. Take your time over it.

Before you hold the ceremony, eat a light meal. Fasting may increase visions but is counter-productive and may make you feel faint or sick.

Have a bath to which a few drops of lavender, chamomile or rose essential oil have been added to gently mark the boundaries of the everyday world. If it is after dark, in the evening or the early morning, light pink or purple candles in the bathroom and swirl the pools of light, visualising them entering your body and filling it with light. When you have finished your bath, blow out the candles, sending the light to whoever needs it, not forgetting yourself. Let the water drain away, saying:

> *Darkness, doubts flow from me,*
> *From the rivers to the sea,*
> *Leaving only harmony.*

Put on something comfortable, but not with flowing sleeves or hem (these would be dangerous as you will be working with open flames). You might like to keep a special close-fitting robe for your formal smudging work.

The ritual of lighting

Sometimes you will want to make your ceremony special, whether you are working alone or in a group. You can open your ritual in the following way, within the centre of your Medicine Wheel, or within your four directional candle circle, or in a visualised circle of light or fire. You can position members of a group around the perimeter of the circle with one at each of the directional points, one in the centre to the left of the smudging tools for Sky and one to the right for Earth. The person who is organising the ritual should stand in the centre. Alternatively, you can take turns to smudge.

* Place the shell or bowl in front of you, in the centre of the circle. If you are using a smudge stick, place it in a container until you are ready to begin.

* Raise the bowl or stick, still unlit, to each of the four directions of the compass, beginning in the East, then to the Sky and finally lower it to the Earth, saying:

> *To all who join their powers with mine/ours and to the*
> *creator/creatrix of this shell/clay/smudge stick,*
> *we give thanks and make these offerings.*

* Return the bowl or stick to the centre.

* Scatter a few herbs or seeds into a small ceramic or wooden offerings bowl or, if you are working out of doors, on to the

ground. You can use the kind of herbs you are smudging with or any others that you know grow well in your region.

* Pick up your smudge stick or your herbs in their container once more and again acknowledge the six directions, saying:

> *For these herbs and their creator/creatrix we give thanks and make these offerings.*

* Scatter a few more herbs or seeds into the bowl or on the ground.
* Next, light the herb mix or the smudge stick from the candle or with matches, saying:

> *Fire to Fire, I/we give thanks to Grandfather Sun, to the lightning flash, to volcanoes and the fires deep within the Earth. I/we greet the Spirit of Fire and thus make this offering.*

* After the ritual, if you did not scatter them on the ground, plant the contents of the offering bowl in a pot and either smudge round it or smudge the earth where the seeds fell, saying:

> *To the Mother we return her own, that life and growth and renewal may ever continue. Blessings be.*

* Now, if you are using a smudge stick, extinguish it by tapping it against the offerings bowl or any glass or ceramic container. If you are using herbs in a bowl, leave them to burn through.

A traditional travel ritual

This ceremony can be used either for yourself or for loved ones who are going on a physical journey or who face difficult times, for example bullying at school or work. If the children are young or the person would feel self-conscious, you can smudge over a photograph or a symbol of them, or you can pass an amulet or lucky charm nine times through the smoke to endow it with protection.

Yet again, the important factor is what you feel in your heart and what you say from the heart and so any words I use are only suggestions. Remember that the great Spirit in the Sky has far more urgent matters to attend to than checking that each suppliant is following a ten-point plan to the letter. But He or She might just understand that you are worried because you have never before had to change trains in a foreign country alone on a business trip, or that no one will take seriously the fact your child is waking crying every night because of teasing at school.

White or grey sage are both good for combining power with protection. Lavender can melt fears and also inflexible attitudes, so you could burn a sage smudge stick in which you have bound sprigs of lavender.

* Light your smudge stick and stand in the centre of a visualised circle of light or your Medicine Wheel. Beginning from the East, smudge a clockwise circle around yourself and a symbol of the journey or problem, for example a suitcase, briefcase or a child's school bag. Say:

Around, surround, may peace abound.

* Raise your smudge to the skies, then lower it to Mother Earth, chanting:

Above and below, may it be so.

* Smudge around the bag or symbol, first anti-clockwise and then clockwise, beginning from the floor and moving upwards and then down in continuous spiralling movements, six times for the six directions, saying:

By the benign protection of the Earth and the all-encompassing power of the Sky, by the winds of the East, the fire of the South, the healing waters of the West and the nurturing womb of the North, guard and guide – (name the person) on this journey/endeavour, returning him/her safely home.

You can smudge around a person (including yourself) in the same way. I am a little apprehensive about smudging fuelled-vehicles for safe journeys because of the fire risk, but you could smudge a symbol that will be carried in the car, for example a St Christopher.

If the amulet or item is small, pass it through the smoke in spiralling movements, holding the smudge stick in the hand you write with, known magically as your power hand.

Smudging other people

Smudging of people is done for all kinds of reasons – protection, cleansing, healing, etc. The exact order and method are not as important as the feeling and the intent, but once again it is something that improves with practice. This is just one example of how to carry this out.

* Begin smudging from the crown, pausing at the brow between the eyes.
* Move in turn to the centre of the throat, the heart, the solar plexus or navel area and lastly the genitals or womb.
* Complete the movement with a general sweep downwards to the feet, coming up via the base of the spine and corresponding points on the back of the body, before ending back at the crown.

(These points on the body correspond with the chakras or psychic energy points that come from the spiritual tradition of the Far East.)

Do what feels right – your hand will guide you in smudging if you do not consciously try to direct it. Smudging is like dancing. Once you stop watching your feet and listen to the beat, you move in time. The order given above does not have to be rigidly applied – some practitioners always smudge the heart before going to the crown. You may find playing Native North American music helps (see page 188 for suggested suppliers). If you are smudging another person, you may find it more natural to sway as you work and move round them.

Remember: 'Anti-clockwise to remove, clockwise to infuse'. This is the only rule to be obeyed when dealing with energies and magic, and whether you start at the head or feet really is your choice. You may like to acknowledge the six directions briefly with your smudge before any smudging ceremony for yourself or others. You, or whoever is leading the ritual, form a seventh direction, or magical focus, and thus can also be smudged now, to receive the blessings of the other six directions.

Smudging yourself

In an earlier ritual, I used a method of smudging people that began at the heart (see pages 63–6). This is another equally valid method for purification, empowerment or healing, this time used on yourself.

∗ Beginning at the left foot, smudge up the left leg with your smudge stick.

∗ Move upwards along the front central column of the body (sometimes called the chakra or psychic energy point line), and clockwise around the top of the head.

∗ Continue down the front central column of the body again and then down the right leg to the right foot.

As you smudge the centre line you can waft the smoke around the back. (If you are smudging another person, you can smudge up the front and down the back.)

You can repeat this a number of times if you wish: three times signifies the sacred triplicate of mind, body and spirit; four times is for balance and the four cardinal directions; six times will include the Sky and Earth; seven times is for the six directions plus yourself; finally, if a matter is acute or urgent, do it nine times – the number of perfection.

The real criterion is what suits the purpose of the ritual. The more urgent the need or the greater the protection and empowerment needed, the more times you should smudge.

Instead of using a smudge stick, you can, if you prefer, smudge yourself with a bowl and fan while kneeling or sitting. (You can smudge others by carrying these items with you as you move round them.)

If a problem is long-standing or acute – for example a really negative atmosphere in a house or workplace, or a habit you find hard to quit – you may need to smudge over a period of days. During this time you can perhaps decrease the purification as the atmosphere lightens and increase the positive or healing energies to replace it. Again, there are no hard and fast rules. If in doubt, test your results with a pendulum (see pages 105–6 and 165–6) and when it spirals clockwise in a place or over a person, you will know the problem is resolved. Then smudge for a final time with an empowering herb such as sage or the gentler sweetgrass.

You can also place your receptive hand (the hand you do not use for writing) in the smoke of the bowl and waft the smoke on to any small area or specific body part that you feel needs extra spiritual or physical healing.

Cupping and centring

Using a smudge stick or a bowl of herbs, you can, literally, make cups of smoke to pour over yourself. This method will remove negativity and tension and enable you to strengthen your essential self to resist all the more easily the pressures of those people and situations that unsettle you. It is also a way of connecting with your inner stillness.

A bowl of broad-leafed sage or a sage and rosemary smudge stick work especially well for this. In group work you can pass the bowl or stick, with each smudging the person on their immediate right. You can scoop the smoke with your receptive hand or, if you put the bowl on the floor or a table, you can use both hands.

* Take the first cup of smoke and surround your heart with it, seeing the essence of the herbs as a golden aura cleansing and empowering, replacing sorrow, pain, stress and anger with harmony and confidence.
* Next take a cup of smoke and gently pass it over the crown of your head and down your neck like a shower, again visualising the

golden light, the essence of the herbs, entering you inner self, clearing troubled thoughts and doubts and replacing them with focus and concentration. You may be aware of white light pouring into the crown of your head from the cosmos once blockages have been cleared by the smoke.

* Using your right hand as a cup, smudge your left arm, then change hands and with your left hand smudge the right arm, seeing the golden aura replacing uncertainty and hesitation with firm but kindly action.

* Cup your navel with smoke, seeing the golden light clearing stagnation and your natural instinctive wisdom replacing unfocused irritability and over-reliance on others.

* Finally, use your left hand to smudge your right leg and foot, then your right hand to smudge your left leg and foot, seeing yourself connected with and grounded in the stability and all-accepting love of Mother Earth. You may be aware of rich, red light rising to merge with the gold and white light from the cosmos. Physical pains and emotional tensions will have ebbed away into the Earth, to be transformed into new beginnings and growth.

A group ritual held on the crescent Moon

Earlier in this chapter I described a group ritual during which people could stand at the six directions (see pages 86–7). In a more elaborate ritual, the six members of the group can greet the wise guardian or power animal of the appointed direction. When working with a group, you will find that different people like to lead specific rituals. Some are naturally good at healing work, others at protective or cleansing ceremonies.

Wish-magic

The night of the crescent Moon is traditionally the night when wishes are granted, and in this ritual each member of a group can ask for what it is they want or need for themselves, for others or for a cause dear to their heart. Smudging is, as I have said, more about receiving blessings spontaneously from the cosmos, but if you are worried about paying the bills or are having housing problems, you are unlikely to be able to tune in spiritually to cosmic energies until your all-essential earthly matters are settled. So it is quite acceptable to use smudging wish-magic to focus on your personal needs or those of your family or close friends. You can also use wish-magic for a particular environmental or peace issue.

This ritual can be a focus for a monthly meeting for friends or family and you can take it in turns to lead it and act out the different roles.

Arrangements for the ritual

Ideally you should have at least seven people for this group ritual. One person will lead the ritual from the centre, and you will need four to invoke the four cardinal directions. They can stand or sit at the four main compass points in a Medicine Wheel or a visualised circle of light. Two more members will represent the Sky and Earth directions, standing or sitting to the left and right of the leader in the centre of the circle respectively. You can adapt the ritual for a smaller number of people by doubling up the roles.

You will also need six candles. Set four round the edge of the circle in the four main cardinal directions (see page 62 for suggested colours) and two more in the centre. This will mark out the circle of light and make it easy for anyone in the group to re-light the smudge if it goes out.

Choose grey sage, if you have it, for your smudge stick or bowl of herbs, for the Moon Mother.

✻ Stand in the centre of the circle and light the smudge stick or bowl, then make a smoke circle around the group clockwise or just inside the Medicine Wheel, beginning in the East, saying:

May the circle that is cast by these sacred herbs remain unbroken. May the Sacred Hoop of existence extend around us all, stones, trees, plants, insects, birds, animals and humans, uniting us in brother- and sisterhood. Blessings be on all gathered within.

✻ Give the bowl or stick to the Guardian of the East, who will then turn to face out of the circle and smudge three clockwise circles, saying:

Wise spirits of the East, we welcome you and ask your protection and blessings.

✻ The Guardian of the East then carries the bowl to the Guardian of the South who greets the spirits of the South and smudges three clockwise circles in the same way.

✻ Continue in this way until the four cardinal directions have been smudged and invoked.

✻ Now the Guardian of the North takes the smudge to the Guardian of the Sky, who is standing in the centre of the circle to the left. The Guardian of the Sky smudges three ascending clockwise circles and asks the blessings of the spirits of the Sky.

✻ The smudge is passed to the Guardian of the Earth, who smudges three descending clockwise circles and asks the blessings of the spirits of the Earth.

✴ The smudge is returned to the centre. The leader then smudges a clockwise circle in the direction of the crescent Moon in the sky (don't worry if it is obscured by clouds) and says:

Lady Moon, we ask that you grant these our requests, that we or those for whom we ask may receive enough for our needs and a little more and that you shower blessings on all who this night call out to you for help or comfort, Goddess of ten thousand names.

You can modify this chant if you are concentrating on a joint environmental project.

✴ Next, each member of the group in turn, beginning with the Guardian of the East and ending with the leader of the ritual, smudges three clockwise circles around his or her heart for the three phases of the Moon and makes a wish, silently if preferred. Pass the smudge clockwise round the circle.

✴ When the smudge is returned to the centre, an offerings bowl is handed round the circle and the members each put in a silver coin, the colour and metal of the Moon, repeating their wishes. The money can be given to charity or used to give pleasure to someone who is ill or unhappy.

Unlike formal magical systems, the smudge circle does not need to be uncast but continues to provide protection even after the group has physically dispersed. However, you may wish to end the ritual, by drawing a huge circle of smoke clockwise in the air and another on the ground. Stand in the centre, saying:

May the Sacred Hoop remain unbroken and all present be united in friendship with those who are in other lands, those who have gone before and those who are yet unborn but who will one day meet in the sacred circle as we do now.

Afterwards you can remain sitting in the circle, passing round food and drink that was prepared beforehand and sharing visions and insights. People often report seeing animals around the circle, even if they are unfamiliar with the tradition, or wise Native North American guardians at the four cardinal points, or a beautiful light above and a deeper red one or rich green grass beneath.

You can use the same casting procedure, if you are working alone, to create your sacred space and wish on the Moon.

Smudging in everyday life

For some people smudging forms a natural beginning to any ritual or act of healing, and they like to use it before a major family conference or one at work. For others it is a natural start to the day – like brushing your teeth.

My friend Dev Hall, who imports and sells Native North American artefacts as well as smudge materials, told me:

Every day I smudge my stock, my workspace and my stall at trade shows. When I cleanse I use prayer feathers to clear unhealthy energy. I begin in the East. Some tribes, for example the Blackfoot, first face the West, the direction of the Thunder Beings. After the four directions, I go up to Grandfather Sky and down to Mother Earth.

Smudging your belongings

You can smudge a room lightly if there are others present who would find the ceremony unsettling. However, learn from my own experience: when I began to smudge secretly, the family were convinced the house was on fire for about three days because of the lingering smoke.

Smudging is a good way to provide protection for yourself and your surroundings. It can be helpful to smudge to cleanse yourself and your home after a quarrel or a confrontational visitor. Beginning at the front door, smudge the step and then go upstairs to the left corner of the room on the left of the top floor of your house. Smudge the four corners of the room, then the centre, towards the ceiling and floor. Work your way down through the house, left to right, smudging all the rooms, until you end at the back door where again you smudge the step. If you live in a flat, you can also smudge communal landings or entrances very lightly if they form boundaries to your home.

Smudging will also cast a cloak of psychic and psychological invisibility around you if you are entering a potentially dangerous or confrontational situation, for example if you have to go out after dark or wait for transport in lonely places. It is also frequently used to cleanse the tools and artefacts of other types of magic, such as crystals.

When smudging objects, smudge yourself first, beginning with the heart and moving upwards and then downwards, finally drawing a circle of smoke waist-high in which to work. If you place the items on a table, you can move easily round them and have both hands free to smudge. You can pass small artefacts, jewellery or crystals through the smoke. Some practitioners use figure-of-eight movements to incorporate the sacred spiral. The spiral is one of the oldest shapes to be painted in the world, and has been found in palaeolithic cave art, where it represents the Mother Goddess (see pages 35–6).

Smudging for self-healing

Finally, smudging is a powerful method of self-healing, invoking the Sacred Plant Spirit Guides. Especially effective is to smudge your aura, the energy field round your body, to cleanse it, clear blockages and restore energy and immunity. You can also heal family and friends with whom you have the necessary emotional and spiritual bond. It is just as effective to smudge people in their absence, using a photograph or one of their treasured possessions to create a psychic link, always with prior permission to avoid infringing free will. This method is especially good for children, pregnant women or those with any respiratory or allergic illness as they do not come into direct contact with the smoke.

Chapter 6
Smudging and healing

Healing within Native North American tradition is all-embracing, for healing, whether it be of an individual or a tribe, was linked with the restoration of balance to the land. Rain dances, for example, were not believed literally to cause rain, but to create the harmony necessary for rain to fall at the appropriate time. In the same tradition, even today, if any part of a person's mind, body or spirit is out of balance, whether it is manifested by physical or emotional illness, treatment is of a holistic kind.

In today's technological west, however, the treatment of physical symptoms has been separated from the treatment of the mind. Physicians deal with the body, psychiatrists deal with the mind, and priests – and latterly New Age practitioners – deal with the spirit, although it must be said this is now slowly changing as each field recognises the importance of the others.

Shamans and smudging

But it is not only in the Native North American world that healing the spirit has always been an integral part of healing. Throughout the world, from Siberia to Africa and in Australian Aboriginal cultures, shamans, the indigenous priest and priestess healer-magicians, heal both individuals and the community when they suffer soul loss.

Shamans travel in spirit bodies to other realms, high in the sky, deep within the earth or below the sea to negotiate with the Mistress of the

Herds or the Fish to release food for the people. They explore the underworld that may be inhabited by talking animals and mythical beasts, where they may find the missing soul or spiritual essence of a person or community who is ill or distressed.

Though we no longer believe in the literal loss of the soul, many of us may at some time suffer a sense of alienation from the world around us, and an inability to relax. We may find we are suffering a number of minor accidents or illnesses that linger long after they should have run their natural course.

And even in our modern world, ordinary people are now finding that by following shaman-style rituals, of which smudging forms an integral part, they are able to reintegrate their whole self. As well as relieving pain or anxiety, shamanic smudging can offer glimpses of the worlds we last saw in fairy tales and occasionally visit in vivid dreams.

In shamanic smudging, fragrant herbs are cast on the fire and the shaman's spirit or etheric body rises on the smoke, ascending the cosmic World Tree that forms the centre of the Earth. This also offers access via deep tunnels or the pool at the base of the World Tree, to the Lower Realms and the Lands Beneath the Sea as well as the Upper Realms of the Wise Spirits.

Altered consciousness

As I suggested on page 90, a state of altered consciousness may follow naturally as you dance or sway while smudging. You can also move rhythmically while kneeling if smudging yourself from a bowl.

But you can heighten this further by incorporating into your smudging rituals a number of methods used by shamans. You will still be fully aware, but may feel as though you are in a light trance in which colours are more vivid, fragrances more powerful and sounds clearer.

You can create your own mantras, each for a different purpose, and these help to keep the rhythm. If working in a group, one person can use a drum or rattle or the whole group may chant and you will find that you enter a light trance state while still being alert to what is going on around you.

It is wise to take care, however. If you feel even slightly dizzy or 'spaced out', put down the smudge stick or bowl in a safe place, cease chanting and drumming and let the ritual draw to a natural close.

Chanting and drumming

Both chanting and drumming can be used to heighten the atmosphere of your ritual. However, only do this if you feel comfortable with it – self-consciousness is not conducive to effective ritual practice. Experiment with different types of chanting until you can produce the kind of sounds you feel are right for you. Visualise golden light emanating from your throat and begin with the lowest note you can comfortably make and then the highest without any undue strain. This is your natural range and you can experiment with sounds and chants that emanate spontaneously.

Shamanic chants frequently use a pentatonic scale, which is made up of five notes instead of the eight in the octave on which our conventional western music is based. You can make up chants using the pentatonic scale by playing only the black notes on the piano, giving you something like the one below:

Try composing some short phrases to chant. You might base these on power animals or spirits that you feel particular affinity for. Your chants might go something like this:

> *Mother Turtle, Father Eagle, hear and heal.*
> *Might of the Father, love of the Mother, might of the Mother,*
> *love of the Father, bless and protect.*
> *Grandfather Hawk, Grandmother Bear, thus I /we entrust*
> *my/our life to thy care.*
> *Moon, Stars and Sun, Earth, Sea and Sky, guardian powers,*
> *hear this our/my cry.*

Once you are happy with your chanting, you can practise it in ritual.

If a drum is being beaten during the smudging ceremony, aim for a steady 240 drumbeats a minute – this corresponds to your brain waves. It also takes account of the lower vibrations of the ear and is considered the single most effective tool for raising consciousness. Rattles or rainsticks affect the higher vibrations of the ear.

Practise chanting in a group, with one person acting as the smudger, wafting smoke over the drummer, the person with the rattle and any dancers; before long you will find you are all moving in harmony.

Gradually slow the chanting and drumming until at last you all fall silent. Sit and gaze into the smoke of the bowl or place the stick in a container and share the visions you experienced. You may be surprised how similar they are, for often shamanic smudging induces a state of collective consciousness.

If you are working alone, you can play a CD of drum music from one of the indigenous cultures and chant along as you dance and smudge yourself and the room. Try naming in your chant any absent friends or family members who may need healing; as you name each one, visualise him or her in front of you and smudge the spirit form.

After you have smudged, gradually slow down and turn down the music so it can hardly be heard. Sit quietly. Let visions form that may shed light on issues in your life.

Healing auras

In the Introduction I explained how the aura, a field of interactive energy that surrounds the body, reflects not only the essential person, but his or her current emotional state, thoughts, desires and anxieties. A person's aura appears as a coloured ellipse that under certain circumstances can be seen psychically, felt or sensed. Auras vary in size and density under different conditions and are estimated to extend from between a few centimetres to approximately the extent of an extended arm span.

The colours of the aura can alter according to the state of health or well-being of an individual and may be observed as radiating, intermingling and swirling bands of colour. Usually one or two colours predominate at a particular time, but some may prevail over months or even years. For example, if you are unwell or stressed, the aura will appear dull with black jagged streaks or dense patches, tears or holes, missing parts or harsh shades.

Your aura can become tangled with the negativity or anxieties of others and may also suffer from pollutants, stress, overwork, junk food and lack of fresh air. The ill-effects of these are seen in the aura before they reach the physical body, and you can remove them by cleansing the aura. There are many ways to do this, but smudging is a particularly effective way of cleansing an auric field of impurities, and of healing imbalances long before they can reach a level at which they may cause physical problems. The same process will give energy and harmony to your body and mind to replace any negativity.

Though some people prefer to cleanse the aura in the morning, the evening before bed is a good time to remove the day's negativity, so that you will enjoy restful sleep and wake naturally energised (see page 181 for suggested books on auras).

Seeing auras

Even without detailed knowledge of auras, you can smudge your aura using the instinctive wisdom we all possess. As children, many of us routinely saw auras or colours around people's heads and bodies. Our reasons for colouring cows blue and cats yellow were not solely due to the limitations of the crayon box but because we saw the essential nature of the creature. Once we had learned that cows must be brown or black or fawn and to trust only our physical senses, the ability to read auras faded, but it is still within us, ready to be awakened. So in a sense you have to forget how *not* to see auras.

To see your aura, look in a mirror with the light behind you. To see the auras of other people, stare hard at them. Close your eyes, open them, blink and describe the aura immediately without analysing your words as you speak. That is invariably the most accurate way of reading an aura.

You can also using coloured pencils or crayons to draw what you see, letting your hand rather than the conscious mind lead you.

To follow the energy flows, hold a pendulum a few centimetres from your head and body. It will swirl anti-clockwise or feel heavy if there is an energy blockage or an area of darkness. Again, draw what you instinctively learn from the pendulum. It is a bit like automatic writing or drawing – you let the unconscious mind dictate the information.

Even if at first you lack confidence in your own intuitive abilities, the aura is self-regulating. As you cleanse it by smudging, the impurities are automatically cleared and, as you energise the aura, again the healing powers will find their target.

Understanding the colours of your aura

Below I have listed briefly the significance of the different colours for mind, body and spirit so that you can recognise them in either your own aura or those of other people – you can even read the auras of animals and places. An area can have a psychic smog or harshness if it has been polluted or used excessively for commercial gain. You can use the colour meanings below to indicate the nature of the problem and then smudge either at the spot or by creating a map of the place and smudging that (see pages 123–4).

In an individual, if the colours that are most visible around the head are pale, discoloured or streaked, they can indicate special areas of the body that may benefit from extra smudging.

White
White is for the life force, enthusiasm, general good health and integration of mind, body and soul. It rules the bones and the immune system. If it is pale or dull, this can indicate physical, mental and spiritual exhaustion or feeling out of touch with people and life in general. If it looks harsh, there can be a danger of burn-out.

Red

Red represents physical strength, energy, courage, efficient blood circulation, healthy cellular growth and sexual potency. However, a murky red aura can indicate general infections, suppressed resentment or anger and blood problems (anaemia may be a dull red), and a harsh red aura points to a high temperature, hyperactivity, panic attacks or high blood pressure.

Red especially refers to the blood and survival mechanism, the spine, the legs and feet.

Orange

Orange shows confidence, joy and fertility. A clear orange aura indicates a regular pulse rate, healthy metabolism and efficient immune system; but cloudy orange can augur allergies, infections in the reproductive system, menstrual pain and sometimes gall-bladder problems. A pale orange can indicate a lack or loss of identity or low self-esteem, while a harsh orange can represent problems with phobias and food-related illnesses.

Orange refers particularly to the ovaries, large and small intestines, spleen, adrenal glands, kidneys and muscles.

Yellow

Yellow represents the mind, clear focus and communication. A clear bright yellow speaks of a good memory, excellent powers of concentration, a well-functioning lymphatic and nervous system and healthy digestion. A dull yellow can indicate digestive and skin disorders, especially those that are stress-related, nervous exhaustion and tension. A harsh yellow can indicate jealousy or repressed venom.

Yellow rules the solar plexus, liver and kidneys, the nervous system and joints where rheumatism or arthritis may occur.

Green

Green is for love, harmony and concern for the environment. A clear green is a sign of a low and stable blood pressure, a healthy heart and respiratory system. Pale green can suggest emotional dependency. A metallic green that flickers expresses a tendency to panic attacks and food-related illnesses, while a murky green can reveal a tendency to coughs and colds, chest infections, viruses and bronchial problems. A dull, muddy green can conceal conflicting emotions or susceptibility to emotional blackmail. Yellowy green can be a sign of possessiveness and unwarranted jealousy.

Green rules the heart, lungs, arms, respiratory system, tissue and cell growth and general body regeneration. If respiratory problems are acute, you should consider using herbal remedies in another form; check with a good herbal book (see page 182) or consult a pharmacist as some smudging herbs are not safe for infusions or taking internally.

Blue

Blue represents idealism, broad vision and integrity. A clear or bright blue is a sign of stable blood pressure, slowing and regulating surges of energy into channelled calm activity, balanced hormones and a regular pulse rate. A dull blue can suggest throat, thyroid or teeth problems or depression; an over-active thyroid is often shown by quite a murky blue. Metallic blue can reveal a tendency towards migraines and headaches, and in children can be an early warning of teething problems.

Blue rules the left side of the brain and the nervous system.

Purple

Purple is for inner vision, psychic awareness and spirituality. A rich clear purple indicates that mind, body and spirit are in harmony and that the physical and psychic senses merge naturally. A dull or cloudy purple can suggest a tendency to eye or ear infections, headaches, insomnia and nightmares. A dark colour may indicate loneliness.

Purple rules the right side of the brain, the eyes and ears, the sinuses, the scalp and all aspects of pregnancy and childbirth.

Pink

Pink represents unconditional love, reconciliation and gentleness. A vibrant pink aura signifies balanced emotions, regular sleep patterns, and the ability to remain relaxed, even in challenging situations, as well as innate healing abilities, especially in children and animals. A harsh pink can reveal a tendency to headaches and earache as well as possessiveness, while a very transparent pink is a sign of physical and emotional exhaustion.

Pink rules the head, glands, all illnesses with psychosomatic origin, eyes, migraines, ear problems and the well-being of the family, especially babies and children.

Brown

Brown is for nurturing powers, for acceptance of frailty in self and others and for grounding. A rich brown is indicative of a store of physical energy and primal strength. A dull shade can indicate an overload of work and stress and blocked or stagnant energies, while a harsh brown can be the aura of someone with money worries.

Brown rules the feet, the hands, the skeleton and the large intestine.

Black

Black is for rest and regeneration. A clear, almost transparent black aura may indicate that a person is resting emotionally and spiritually, perhaps after an exhausting or stressful period, and so is growing stronger behind the protective darkness. Because psychic protection is so strongly implicated in a positive black aura, its possessors may deliberately or spontaneously be shielding themselves from intrusion. A matt black indicates exhaustion or depression, but is more usually seen as black spots or streaks than as a blanket aura. However, a harsh, metallic black can suggest that the person is potentially a psychic vampire, who will offload problems, but ignore any positive suggestions and put the most negative interpretation on the motives and actions of others.

The presence of black spots in the aura may indicate that some part of the body is imbalanced or that energies are not flowing freely. This may mean that the person has some negative habits that he or she should work on.

Black, like brown, rules the feet, the legs, the bones and the large intestine.

A ritual for healing the aura

Once you have identified problems in the auric field, you can begin to cleanse the whole body and auric field around the body. I have listed suitable healing herbs on pages 114–19 and 166–79 but you can experiment to find those that are best suited to you.

Arrangements for the ritual

You can heal with a herb that has both cleansing and empowering properties. White or grey sage or any of the sagebrushes are excellent for all forms of healing, as are sweetgrass and cedar.

Alternatively, you can mix separate cleansing and empowering herbs in a bowl or first use your purification herbs and then the restorative ones in individual smudge sticks, or in a bowl followed by a stick. For example, if you want to help cure frequent migraines, you could use specific herbs such as mint or lavender or an all-healer such as sweetgrass, visualising the essence of the herb as either golden light or a colour related to the herb, directed towards the source of the pain, and melting it away. You can also use incense sticks or granular incense for healing.

Do check when burning herbs for healing if they are unfamiliar to you that they will not have any adverse effects on someone whose immune system may be temporarily weakened. All herbs have healing properties and if you cannot find a suitable herb for a particular disorder, use general purpose ones that conduct the life force. If in doubt use sage.

* Begin by thanking the herbs for offering their healing powers with such words as:

To you who offer your greening power to purify and uplift, I give thanks; to Grandfather Sun and Mother Earth who have warmed and nurtured these sacred herbs, to the winds that have breathed into them life and power, to the Moon who has filled them with her silver wisdom, the wise Grandfathers and Grandmothers who stood sentinel around the Hoop of existence that they might grow safe and unpolluted, I offer blessings.

Smudging and incense burning

* Since the aura you see is an extension of the spirit body that is within the physical one, it is best to start with a general cleansing, and if the aura is indicating total exhaustion or stress everywhere then this will be sufficient. As you work, chant or invoke silently the kind of healing you need from the cosmos or the Earth, using the herbs as a channel.

* Fan the smoke over the affected area of the body or aura. You can use feathers to fan a bowl of herbs as feathers are especially good for combing out auric tangles and spreading healing energies. Let the patient sit or lie with the bowl nearby so you can fan the smoke. If you are using charcoal, make sure the patient cannot get burned. Smudge sticks are also potent and you can give the patient a feather fan to spread the smoke.

* Smudge anti-clockwise from the top of the body downwards in spirals, remembering to extend the smudge to as far as you can detect the aura. Then go down a second time, this time swirling over the specific problem areas.

* If you are healing someone else, you can ask them to identify specific areas of the body where there is pain or discomfort. You can cleanse these on your second pass over the body and visible auric field. However, if for example you detected that there was a dull yellow tinge to the aura or perhaps even around the navel area (some people can see the rainbow colours of the inner body), you should smudge the stomach area. Note that although the sufferer might be complaining of headaches, the aura reading may indicate that the cause is residing in the stomach, so this is the area you concentrate on.

You may find that at certain points the smudge feels resistant. This is a blockage and you may need to make several anti-clockwise swirls. As you work, visualise darkness and heaviness flowing from the body into the Earth.

* Now you can restore the energies by smudging upwards from the feet, this time with a clockwise spiral, following the aura outline and ending with a clockwise circle over the crown of the head.

* Returning to the feet, spiral upwards clockwise a second time, pausing and smudging an extra clockwise circle at the areas of discomfort. Fill in any holes or missing parts of the aura with the smoke. See light flowing from all round, in rainbow colours, energising and enriching.

* End with a final clockwise circle around the crown of the head.

* After the ceremony, extinguish the smudge stick and herbs, saying:

For blessings received from the Earth, the Sky and the Great Spirit (or name your own god/goddess form), we give thanks and ask your continuing healing, help and protection. May the sacred circle remain unbroken.

With the patient, plant a few seeds or seedlings in a pot, adding a moss agate or jade to the soil, and give it to the patient as a symbol of the continuing process of restoration and new life.

When the patient has gone home, remember to cleanse your smudging tools and yourself, as well as the room if you are working indoors (see page 98) so that any lingering negativity is absorbed by the cosmos and the Earth.

You can heal yourself in the same way for general and specific illnesses.

Herbs for healing

The following herbs are those you will be familiar with from the previous chapters, but here I have concentrated on their specific healing properties. You can, of course, heal with any of the basic herbs – for example, cleansing with cedar and empowering with sweetgrass or using sage with either of these two. Though the smoke of the herbs does contain some of the goodness and specific properties, the healing takes place primarily on the spiritual level. The essence of the herbs is transferred through the act of smudging into golden, healing light, which you visualise filling specific areas of the body that are painful or tense. As well as golden or rainbow light, some especially clairvoyant healers have detected a rich green. This was referred to by the eleventh-century German mystic Hildegard von Bingen as *veriditas* or 'the greening process'. You may find it helpful to visualise this green light emanating from your smudge stick or bowl as you work.

Do not smudge in pregnancy or if you suffer from certain conditions (see page 13).

If in doubt as to which herb to smudge, hold your pendulum over a number of herbs, or even a list, and ask it to indicate a suitable choice. It will do this by pulling downwards or moving in a clockwise circle over the most appropriate one to use in smudging. This method accesses your inner wisdom and is often an accurate indication of factors of which the conscious mind is not aware (see pages 105 and 123).

Bay
A purifier and gentle uplifter, it eases depression and anxiety, helps with digestive and joint problems and assists a weight-loss programme; it is also good for relieving food-related disorders.

Cedar
Cedar removes all forms of negativity and offers psychic protection. A symbol of long-life, it is said to help with eczema and other nervous skin complaints and any stress-related symptoms. It is effective against fluid retention and for awakening sexual potency.

Chamomile
The most gentle and soothing of herbs, chamomile relieves anxiety, insomnia, and gastric and menstrual problems. It is also good for eye problems and congestion after colds. It is a natural relaxant and is very protective.

Juniper
Cleansing and protective, juniper is a natural antiseptic, and also soothes digestive and gastrointestinal inflammations, kidney problems, arthritis and rheumatism. It strengthens the body's natural anti-inflammatory mechanisms.

Lavender

The true all-healer, lavender has both calming and restorative properties. It is an anti-depressant, a natural sedative and a pain reliever, especially good for tension-related headaches and muscle or joint pains. It also helps digestion and brings peaceful sleep, preventing irritability, harshness and hyperactivity.

Mint

Mint is both a purifier and an empowerer, good for relieving all forms of nausea and sickness, menstrual problems, headaches, migraines and digestive disorders. Note that the more mint you burn, the more potent it is as an energiser, whereas a thin stream of smoke will promote relaxation and peaceful sleep. It removes all negativity from self and home.

Mugwort

Cleansing and protective, mugwort reduces stress and tension and relieves depression. It is good for all digestive and menstrual problems. It is also a good all-purpose healer and is effective for the integration of the mind with higher consciousness.

Orris root

Naturally protective, orris root drives away fears and deflects malevolence. It is good for skin disorders, for improving memory, for problems with self-esteem and self-love and for issues of ageing. However, it is now not generally used medicinally for physical ills.

Pine
Purifying and protective, pine relieves anxiety, fatigue, insomnia, skin problems and joint disorders and speeds the healing of physical and mental wounds. It removes all negativity from self and home.

Rose
Rose is the gentle healer and uplifter after sorrow, removing fear, anxiety, grief and unresolved anguish from the past, especially from childhood. It is good for all skin disorders and gall-bladder and digestive problems and is helpful in cases of physical and emotional exhaustion. It is an excellent herb to smudge during the menopause.

Rosemary
Rosemary both cleanses and empowers, relieving headaches and depression, and aiding digestion and the healthy functioning of the liver and gall bladder. It also improves circulation and memory and clarifies and focuses thinking processes. Rosemary increases passion.

Sage

Sage can be used for any kind of healing work. Both cleansing and empowering, sage is good for fertility and for stimulating the balanced flow of the life force. It is also potent for boosting the immune system, helping to build up resistance against colds and coughs for those who are prone to them, and for speeding recovery in debilitating or chronic conditions. Sage eases headaches and menstrual and menopausal problems. It lifts depression and soothes anxieties, and improves memory and the ability to concentrate.

Sweetgrass

Sweetgrass is gently healing and uplifting. It is good for women's disorders and for any hormonal imbalances whether in adolescence, menstruation or the menopause. It releases mental anguish and helps the healing process of old sorrows. It brings fertility and abundance and is good with all addictions, obsessions and compulsions.

Thyme

Very protective and also empowering, thyme heals wounds and treats all fungal infections, digestive disorders and infections of the throat, mouth and gums. It improves memory and metal acuity, especially in older people or those under stress, and relieves insomnia, helps to prevent nightmares and gives the courage to face and overcome fears and foes.

Yarrow

This is a natural relaxant and good for all digestive disorders. Its antiseptic properties and its association with long-term commitments make it good for regeneration of despoiled areas and saving endangered species.

Chapter 7
Smudging for Protection

Smudging is one of the easiest and most potent methods of both physical and psychic protection. You can protect yourself, your home, those you love and your possessions. You can also send guardian energies to any areas or species that may be under threat by smudging around a photograph or symbol. It is also very effective if you feel yourself under psychic attack. This need not be a deliberate assault of any sort, but simply the negativity of someone who is jealous or gossips about you, thus releasing bad feelings in your direction. The result can be that you feel exhausted or have a series of minor illnesses. In Chapter 6 on healing, I suggested ways you could cleanse your aura of impurities. This is a very good way of maintaining ongoing psychic self-defence and works in much the same way as a bath when you come home to wash off both the physical dirt and the tensions of your day.

A special smudging ceremony can be helpful when you buy something new, to protect it from theft and malfunction, if it is mechanical. On page 46 I suggested a cleansing ceremony for tools that can also be used for crystals or jewellery, to remove the vibrations of other people (see also page 98).

You can also smudge your boundaries to protect yourself and your belongings from harm – perhaps when you move house or if your neighbours change, or if there is building work in the immediate vicinity or a spate of burglaries or vandalism. (See also pages 30–3 for clearing your home of a run of bad luck or anger.) The ritual given here is also effective when you move into a newly built home, as sometimes a plot of land upon which even new houses stand can have all kinds of lingering influences and memories from its past use.

A house protection ritual

If you are able to walk all the way around your home, you can smudge its boundaries. If not, smudge around the doors and windows of every room. In this ritual, you are not working at the heart of the home but at the extremities. Do not carry out this ritual if it is windy.

Arrangements for the ritual

Use any two herbs from cedar, juniper, thyme, sage and pine as a smudge stick or in a bowl with a lip or handle that will stay cool while you carry it. Alternatively, use a sage smudge stick.

Position a small outdoor candle or fire in a safe place outside the house, so you can re-light the smudge stick if it goes out.

∗ Light the smudge just inside the front door and smudge around the doorstep, saying:

I call on the Guardian Spirits, the wise ancestors and the protectors of this land for blessing on this sanctuary and all who dwell herein. I ask that you will stand sentinel day and night throughout the seasons and the years.

∗ Carry the smudge around the outside of the house, encircling it in protective smoke. If the smudge stick goes out, re-light it from the candle or fire, then return to the place you last smudged and make a double clockwise loop to join the earlier protection and continue.

Smudging and incense burning

* Now smudge the inside of your house. This time leave a candle in the heart of the house (see page 31) for re-lighting and again return to the place the smudge went out, rejoining the energies with a double clockwise loop. Even if you cannot smudge the boundaries, this internal smudging will protect the whole of your domain.

* Carry your smudge into every room, beginning at the front door with the step, going first upstairs if there is an upper storey, beginning from the top left of the house and working to the top right, then downstairs, from left to right downstairs, ending at the back door. In each case smudge the door, the edges of the room including the windows, beginning in the left corner as you enter and ending in the right one nearest the door by which you came in.

* Then go to the centre of the room and smudge upwards and downwards before leaving the room (see pages 32–3). Make anti-clockwise spirals of smoke, saying in each area:

Let nought harm nor terrify, taunt nor destroy this my refuge. Leave only light and goodness, friendship and blessedness.

* If there is a basement, cleanse it immediately after the ground floor, ending at the back door. Remember to include any balconies or outbuildings. If you live in an apartment you can adapt the ritual, and if there is only one entrance begin and end at that. As it is so heavily used, this portal will benefit from a double smudge.

* Leave the smudge near the front door to burn through and then bury the remains in a small wooden box with a sprig of fresh rosemary and some iron nails for protection, as near to the front door as possible or in greenery on a balcony.

* If you still feel vulnerable, sweep through the air of each room with

fresh cedar, juniper or pine branches, saying:

Begone hence all danger from stranger, from foes familiar and unknown darkness and enter no more.

∗ Burn the branches or shake them outside to remove negativity.

Smudging the workplace

In practice, unless you own the firm, it is not easy to smudge a workplace. Apart from any objections your fellow-workers may raise, you may not be able to de-activate smoke alarms and have the privacy to avoid the curiosity and scepticism of any cynical onlookers – who are usually the ones giving off the most negative vibes.

However, modern workplaces do benefit from smudging. As well as the vibes created by daily interactions and the pollution of any electronic equipment, your place of work may also be built on land where there has been sorrow or exploitation. I have noticed this myself in areas of the now regenerated London Docklands. There may also be stagnant earth energies that need clearing. For more about this, read my book *Psychic Protection Lifts the Spirit* (see page 183).

If you wish to smudge your workplace discreetly, there is a way to avoid unwanted interference: you simply draw your office and smudge over the picture – this is just as effective as walking the floors. You can do this because psychic and spiritual powers do not need direct physical correspondences. That is why it is possible for dowsers to hold a pendulum over a map and discover the precise location of a lost object or water in the material world or to heal a person by dowsing over a diagram of the body.

Arrangements for the ritual

Make a large representation of your workplace on flame-retardant paper. You can use different sheets set one above the other on a flat surface to indicate the various floors or departments. Include lifts, doors, windows and partitions, and label the various desks or workbenches and their occupants, allowing your unconscious mind to shade in any areas in which there is darkness or jagged energies. You can pay especially attention to these. Alternatively, draw the plan on sand or in the earth with a stick or in chalk on an uncarpeted floor or yard.

Use sage or sage and lavender for the ritual as the interactions may be quite complex and so gentle healing may be helpful as well as cleansing. A bowl and fan that you can place off the plan are safest, but you can use a smudge stick if you are careful about hot sparks.

* Light the smudge, saying:

> *May peace alone remain and harmony; though many meet, let*
> *enmity be none and quarrels be gone.*

* As with the house cleansing (see pages 31 and 121), begin from the top, including the lift door or staircase from where negative energies can filter. Work from the entrance in a square but this time move with the smoke inwards to any desks or work stations in clockwise spirals, saying:

> *Be calm, naught harm, be still,*
> *Good will enter,*
> *Peace centre.*

* Smudge downwards, paying particular attention to any dark or jagged areas and putting a clockwise circle of protection around your own work area.

* Finally draw a clockwise circle round the whole area you have smudged, saying:

Keep light always within.

* Place the plan where it will remain clean and uncreased so that you can re-smudge whenever tensions arise.

* Keep a small dish of unburned sage and lavender herbs in your workplace. These are very protective herbs, even when unburned, and can offer protection at times when you cannot smudge.

A ritual to cleanse work tools or equipment

If you have a new computer, a fax machine or a personal item that is of value, smudging can offer protection against theft, accidental damage and gremlins in the works.

* Simply smudge around it with a sage or cedar stick in nine anti-clockwise circles.

* If the item is small you can pass it nine times anti-clockwise through the smudge smoke, saying:

From damage, theft, malicious stranger, from careless use, abuse or flaws within, I ask protection and pledge this artefact/computer will be used only for good intent.

* Allow the stick to burn through in a safe place where the smoke will continue to waft over the item.

A ritual to protect pets against attack or theft

On a whole, animals do not like to have smoke wafted at them as it brings to the fore their instinctive fear of fire. Therefore it is better to smudge round your pet's collar, bed or photograph.

* Light sweetgrass or sage and lavender smudge sticks or sweetgrass and sage in a bowl, visualising as you do so your pet running through the fields or bathed in sunlight.

* Create the nine anti-clockwise circles, saying:

Come not near, you who wish harm, beyond this ring of fire remain, you who would hurt or intrude upon this safe domain.

* Follow this with a clockwise circle of smoke saying:

Bless, protect and preserve this beloved creature and all who need like care and conservation.

A protective ritual to drive away fears or malevolence

On pages 88–90 in Chapter 5, I briefly described ways of protecting yourself and your loved ones. However, sometimes you may feel the need for a special ritual, as you perhaps did when you were a child to drive away night fears, especially if you are under a great deal of stress. It may be that someone is being spiteful or hostile even if they are hiding it when you meet, so you may find yourself suffering inexplicable panic attacks or insomnia as you pick up their hostility.

The following traditional prayer comes from the Kabbalistic, or esoteric Judaic, tradition and bears may similarities to the Christian Lord's Prayer. However, this version allows you to focus on your own source of benign higher protection, which may be a force rather than a specific goddess or god form. I have found that smudging while you say the words adds to the protective power it offers. I have adapted the words for modern usage.

Arrangements for the ritual

If you prefer, you can write your own prayer of protection. You can use any smudge stick you wish, holding it fairly close to your body.

Perform the ritual very slowly, enunciating each word and visualising the cross of light forming within you. Address the form of divinity with whom you are most comfortable or visualise a huge white light radiating all around you.

＊ Light your smudge and raise it so that you waft smoke in the centre of your forehead, saying:

> *As Thou art divine light and protection, so do I draw within me*
> *that light and love.*

❋ Bring your smudge stick down in a straight line, visualising it as a shaft of light and wafting the smoke over your genitals or womb, saying:

As thou art a secure kingdom on Earth, so am I connected and rooted safe within that kingdom.

❋ Lift the stick so the smoke wafts over your right shoulder and say:

As thou art Guardian and Power, so am I protected from all harm by thy enfolding might.

❋ Waft the stick and smoke across to touch your left shoulder and say:

As thou art the Glory, so am I freed from fear by that Glory and Magnificence.

❋ Hold the smudge stick in both hands in front of you so that the smoke flows over your heart and say:

For ever and ever.

❋ Finally extend your hands and arms to form a cross and with your power hand waft the smoke in an arc over your head as you say either Aum (the 'om' sound that according to Buddhists and Hindus brought the universe into being) or Amen.

Auric invisibility

There may be times when you need to be less visible in situations or places in which you are vulnerable. Most ancient invisibility spells relied not on making the physical body actually disappear, but on lowering a person's profile, creating an aura of 'greyness' if you like, so that he or she could walk unnoticed in places of potential danger.

However much we may try to avoid such things, it is inevitable that occasionally we may be left to lock up an empty workplace late in the evening, or have to return to a deserted car park. We may have to wait on a station late at night or try to summon a taxi in an area in which there are drunks or gangs of troublemakers. There are also occasions when it is better to maintain a low profile while learning the dynamics of the situation, and times when you simply do not wish to be drawn into confrontation.

We often know about such situations in advance and so can smudge our aura the evening or morning before to adopt our cloak of greyness. But it is also possible to store up this power for vulnerable moments when you can instantly call up the protection by visualising the smoke. You can also smudge on behalf of others.

A ritual to make you less visible

* Sit in a comfortable position and close your eyes.
* Light a bowl of any easily burned herb. I find that grey sage works best of all for invisibility rituals.
* Sit in front of the bowl fanning gently and visualising the circle of swirling colours around your head and body.
* Fan the smoke up over your body and around your head so that gradually a gentle grey mist descends and the aura fades from your psychic vision.
* Extinguish the bowl with sand or by covering it, and shake yourself like a puppy in a shower of rain. Your aura will now be bright again, but you have the greyness in reserve.
* Whenever you are entering a difficult or potentially dangerous situation, visualise your smudge bowl and the smoke rising. It may help to carry a few of the unburned herbs in a tiny purse and sniff them to recall the fragrance.

I can confirm the success of this method. Joe, a friend of mine, had to go into an office where he had formerly worked, to fulfil a day's freelance contract. Although he was a good worker he had many jealous enemies in that office. He wanted simply to go in, do the job, get paid and come home again without meeting any of the old adversaries.

I offered to carry out my invisibility ritual and duly lit the bowl of sage about ten minutes before he was due to go into the building. Then the phone rang and I left the bowl on a metal tray in the middle of the room where it would be safe. Breaking all my own rules, I forgot it. Ten minutes later I went back into the room to find it filled with thick, grey smoke and had to open all the doors and windows to clear the air. However, when I spoke to Joe later in the day, he was delighted. He had had to work in a booth close to people with whom he had been in conflict but, amazingly, he was not noticed.

What is more, Joe is not the most tolerant of souls, but he found he was able to ignore their loud, unpleasant behaviour echoing round the room. In fact, he finished the job in record time.

Chapter 8
Smudging with Incense

I ncenses offer a vast range of fragrances in stick, rope or cone form that you can substitute for a smudge stick. You can also burn granular incense on charcoal in a bowl of sand or salt or in a censer.

The sticks, cones and ropes are of a combustible, or self-lighting, incense and the granular type is non-combustible.

Smudging incenses

The word 'incense' originally referred to the aroma of any fragrant substance but over the centuries it has become especially associated with special ceremonial fragrances, such as frankincense and myrrh, that are burned on charcoal. (Frankincense and myrrh, with their Sun and Moon energies, are becoming increasingly popular for smudging rituals and when burned together balance conscious awareness with intuitive wisdom.)

In incense, the roots, bark, leaves and flowers of traditional smudging herbs are mixed with a gum resin such as frankincense, dragon's blood, gum arabic (acacia gum) or copal. Copal resin has been used for thousands of years in Central and South American smudging rituals, burned on hot coals or charcoal. It is very rich and aromatic and banishes all negativity, replacing it with light and loving energies. It is also lit before and during healing to drive away pain and sorrow. Incenses containing larger amounts of resins and gums do burn longer than those with leaves or flowers, but may not seem so appropriate for rituals in the open air or those concerning environmental issues.

Essential oil is sometimes added to improve the fragrance.

You can burn non-combustible incense on a charcoal disc or briquette in a bowl half-filled with sand, soil or salt. But a large variety of censers for incense is available and it is well worthwhile studying pictures on the internet or going to a large New Age shop so that you can see which are suitable.

If your incense bowl is sufficiently deep, you can stand the incense sticks in the sand or earth, or you may choose a taller container with a handle so that you can carry the sticks round in ritual. Heatproof ceramic vases are excellent for carrying incense sticks.

Using incense in smudging

You use incense in exactly the same way as herbs for smudging. You can pass objects or crystals through the smoke to purify them, use the fragrance to cleanse your home or yourself of negativity, heal and empower. The words you speak and the fragrance you use will direct the purpose and attract the appropriate energies.

A number of incense sticks do have handles attached that do not burn and so if the incense stick is sufficiently large, stable and solid, you can use it exactly as you would a smudge stick. On a whole, it is worth buying the more expensive sticks for smudging as they will not crumble when you are holding them.

Because all incenses are resinous, they give a richer, more consistent smoke than herbs and do not go out so easily. Smudging with incense sticks is the easiest and most instant form of smoke magic because you have many different fragrances to enable you to focus quite precisely on a specific need or aim. It also means that because the igniting material has already been added to the stick, you can instantly perform a ritual just by lighting the end of the stick, without wondering whether or not the substance will burn without charcoal or waiting for the herbs to smoulder.

Another advantage of smudging with incense rather than herbs is that you can tell from the unburned incense – especially in stick or cone form – the exact fragrance that will be emitted on lighting.

What is more, with sticks and cones it is easy to work out the exact proportions of each herb you need for a ritual, so you can weight the emphasis of the magical intention in any way you like without having the bother of measuring out heaps of herbs.

So, for example, if you are smudging to increase love in your life, perhaps with a specific relationship in mind, you could, if you wanted to encourage gentle spiritual love, burn three rose incense sticks or two of rose and one of lavender. (You can, of course, light as many or as few sticks as you wish but I tend to use three in solo rituals.)

If, however, you wanted to inject passion while preserving underlying tenderness, one of the three sticks could be cinnamon or ginger. For a relationship going through a bad patch or if your guilty, unfaithful lover or partner is being unkind, you might burn two bay or basil sticks for fidelity and one of lavender for kindness and gentleness. (This assumes, of course, that you consider it worth continuing with the relationship!) You might in this case also cleanse your home regularly with bay to clear the negativity and induce fidelity, and then burn your lavender or rose sticks of love, and perhaps cinnamon for love and passion in the bedroom.

Using combustible and non-combustible incense

Combustible incense gives instant results. With sticks, you just light the tip with matches or a taper, blow out the flame once the tip is glowing and the smoke will last up to half an hour, long enough for most rituals. (You can also purchase special garden incense sticks for outdoor rituals.)

With combustible incense ropes and cones, you light one end and burn two or three on a flat smudging dish, using your fan or hands to waft the smoke.

It is possible to make your own combustible incense sticks, but it is very complicated and messy and few people would want to bother.

Non-combustible incense is smouldered on charcoal in the same ways as herbs (see pages 37–9) and the lighting process is exactly the same. Once the charcoal has stopped sparking and is white hot, you can add your incense. The key to incense burning on charcoal – and indeed to using charcoal with any herbs – is moderation. Half a teaspoonful added to the block will instantly produce consistent rich smoke, but if you add too much the block will go out. You can add more as it burns, as part of the ritual, if necessary scraping the ash off the block with the back of the spoon. Keep a special spoon for this – look in antique shops and at car boot sales for the old-fashioned, often ornate, sugar spoons that are even smaller than conventional teaspoons.

You can make your own non-combustible incense, though it does take time and practice to get the procedure right; but those who do say it adds magic to any ritual. The best book with step-by-step instructions is by the late Scott Cunningham and I have given details on page 182.

If you have a holder that collects the ash, you can scatter this to the four winds after the ritual to carry your wishes on their way.

Empowering your incense

Traditionally, practitioners would empower their incense as they made it, by grinding herbs, flowers, berries or leaves with a mortar and pestle, while concentrating on their magical intentions and reciting a mantra. You can do this just as easily with ready-bought incense.

If you use powdered or granulated incense, mix it in a ceramic bowl with a non-metallic spoon, repeating your magical intention and the prime focus of the incense over and over again, faster and faster. You can also empower your incense sticks or cones by placing them in the container in which you are going to burn them and chanting over the container as you turn it nine times clockwise.

So, for example, if you are planning a journey, say:

Fern, fern, let me travel.

As you do so, visualise yourself at your chosen destination in as vivid detail as possible.

You can easily combine two or three fragrances in the empowerment, adding to your chant as you include each new ingredient.

If you want to travel overseas on a business trip intended to win contracts or to find a new job, you might have a three-part chant, for example:

Fern, fern let me travel,
Frankincense, frankincense, cross land and sea,
Cinnamon, cinnamon, there to find the success/position I desire.

Combination effects of incenses

Sometimes a fragrance can have dual or even triple focuses that may be related and you will find that you experience a general increase in all the related areas. For example, if you wanted to increase courage, you would use fennel in a ritual and you would name this property in both the empowerment and the ritual itself. However, fennel is also effective in keeping away unwanted visitors – everything from rodents to aggressive door-to-door salespeople, critical neighbours and all forms of external hostility. So as well as having the courage to meet new challenges and overcome any obstacles, you might notice that the office gossip was, thankfully, steering clear of your workspace. In the same way, since money-making incenses such as allspice also increase passion, your sexual magnetism should improve along with your wealth.

A ritual with two incenses

Use two large and very solid incense sticks with contrasting properties, one to cleanse or take away the negativity and one to empower (see pages 138–40 for good combinations). For example, if you wanted to break a run of bad luck with money you would cleanse with a vetivert or pine incense stick, followed by basil or patchouli to get the prosperity energies flowing.

This ritual is excellent if executed out of doors using large garden incense wands, which create huge circles of smoke. (These larger sticks are also good for marking external boundaries.)

✳ Light both the incenses and leave them in a tall container on a table or tree stump where you can reach them easily.

✳ First waft the vetivert or pine cleansing incense anti-clockwise, upwards from your feet in spirals, followed by an anti-clockwise circle round the crown of your head to banish negativity. Create a cleansing chant, for example:

> *Harsh fortune depart,*
> *Pine take away this bad luck trailing after me.*

✳ Next the positive energies of the basil or patchouli are swept downwards, beginning with a clockwise circle over your crown and ending with another at your feet.

✳ For the empowering cycles you could say:

> *Basil, bring prosperity,*
> *Confidence and opportunity.*

✳ Repeat the cycle twice more, first with vetivert or pine followed by basil or patchouli, ending after the third cycle with a final upwards sweep of the empowering incense with a triple clockwise circle at the crown, saying:

> *Blessings be.*

You can, if you feel in need of an extra infusion of confidence, use empowering incenses in both parts of the smudging ritual. For example, orange is good incense for increasing trust and optimism and is especially related to marriage and permanent relationships. Vanilla is the fragrance of committed love and fidelity.

✳ So as you smudge first downwards and anti-clockwise with orange you might ask:

> *Let doubts and fears recede, leaving only joy and optimism.*

❋ Then, as you work upwards and clockwise with vanilla, you could ask:

Let trust and commitment daily grow, flourish and remain ever so.

Paired incenses

As I said earlier, you can use specific pairs of incenses that combine well to give a desired effect. Below I have listed some of these matching pairs. Burn them in the order I have given.

As well as incense sticks, you can also use cones or ropes in separate dishes or two granular incenses in two dishes. For these you will need a fan. In the list of 65 herbs on pages 166–80 you will find substitutes with similar properties for any of the paired incenses you cannot obtain.

For breaking stagnation or an impasse
Eucalyptus: To clear the blockage
Ginger: The explorer incense, to expand horizons

To find new love after betrayal
Benzoin: To soothe away old hurts
Rose: To bring gentle love

To help with an examination or to learn a new skill
Lemon: To clear away inertia and unfocused thinking
Thyme: To improve memory

To protect your home and family from spiteful neighbours, burglary or vandalism
Hyssop or lemongrass: To mark out the boundaries beyond which harm cannot come
Lilac: To bring love and happiness to the home

To bring fertility and abundance into your life
Dragon's blood: To burn away sterility
Orange blossom: To create fertility in every way

For regeneration of the environment and to fight pollution
Nutmeg: To cleanse and heal what has been spoiled or polluted
Patchouli: To bring new life and to restore growth

To foster reconciliation in a personal quarrel or peace between opposing factions
Myrrh: To heal all wounds, sorrows, anger and resentment
Rosewood: To initiate forgiveness, peace and new bonds

To bring success to a new business venture or life change
Citronella: To break through limitations and obstacles
Frankincense: For assured success

To improve health after illness or exhaustion
Mint: For cleansing the aura of ill-health
Lime or mandarin: To increase well-being

To overcome grief or loss and move towards a new beginning
Cypress: For carrying away grief
Mimosa: For the establishment of peace and gentle optimism

Chapter 9
Smudging for Empowerment

Though smudging is traditionally associated with cleansing, it is a very powerful way of filling your life with light and energy. As I mentioned in the previous chapter, you should concentrate on these positive aspects, asking as you smudge that any doubts, fears or misfortune are transformed into energy for change, joy and abundance.

You can reverse a run of bad luck and attract money, success or love by getting the energies around you moving again if you have been through a period of stagnation or faced opposition to your plans.

Smudging in the sunlight at dawn or noon carries your smoke on light beams into the cosmos and with it your hopes, desires, dreams and intentions. As the smoke swirls, watch it rising in ever-ascending clockwise circles above any obstacles or inertia. If you position your smudge bowl or stick carefully, you can catch the light in the rising smoke, so that it becomes quite golden. If it is a dark time of year, you can use fibre-optic lamps or golden candles to illuminate your smoke.

Smudging for wishes

This is one of the most effective ways of transforming a wish from the thought plane into action.

Arrangements for the ritual

Prepare a bowl of herbs; white sage is best, but if you prefer you can light frankincense or honeysuckle, which are associated with worldly achievement. You can smudge for wishes at either dawn or noon, and on the crescent or full Moon. If working by moonlight, try to catch the full moonbeams in the smoke, or add lots of silver candles if the light is pale. I have set the ritual in sunlight, which I prefer, but you can adapt the words accordingly to refer to moonlight.

If you are using herbs burned on charcoal, you can spend the time while it is heating meditating to raise your psychic awareness (see page 155). Light frankincense or sandalwood incense sticks to increase this.

* Prepare your bowl of herbs and as you add the flame, say:

Flame high, flame true and carry my wishes to the cosmos, that they may enter into the light and become manifest.

* Concentrate on one specific project or wish and, as the herbs begin to smoulder, describe the fulfilment of your dream in as much detail as you can, as though it were a three-dimensional scene in front of you. Be specific about not only the images, but also the sounds and fragrances, whether they are of a place, an object, a person or a new career.

* Choose one or two unburned herbs or a few granules of incense to represent your wish and place them in a ceramic dish.

* Hold this dish with one hand above the main bowl of incense and fan the smoke over it, saying:

The greater is joined to the lesser and carries it high into the celestial spheres. So rise my dreams and cascade as brilliant light beams of fulfilment.

* Put down the bowl and take half the herbs or incense from the small dish. Cast them into the smoke, saying:

The lesser is joined to the greater; it flames and flares, infusing me with the power to make my wish come true.

* Smudge yourself clockwise from heels to head, downwards then upwards for a third time, ending with the triple clockwise circle over your crown, reciting your wish over and over again.
* Take the second half of the wish herbs and cast them into the smoke, saying:

So fires my wish to fulfilment, so it grows and surrounds me with joy that I will not, cannot, fail in this most fortunate venture.

* Smudge clockwise upwards three times; this time when you have reached the crown for the third time, bring the smoke down and enclose yourself in a triple circle, waist-high, saying:

Up, down, around,
light now surround,
enfold, uplift and multiply,
from Earth to Sky, wishes fly.

* Sign your name in smoke in the air as an affirmation of your intention to succeed and leave the smudge to burn away, while planning the first steps to bringing your dreams into reality.

Smudging and Sun signs

Each herb is ruled by both a planet and a Sun sign. By using a specific smudge herb on the day of the week or in the Sun-sign period during which it is most powerful, you can increase the particular magical strength of the herb or incense. You can also combine the herbs. So, for example, if you were taking an examination or an assessment for promotion, you could combine Mercury herbs for learning and Jupiter herbs for promotion.

Also you can, by using your own Sun-sign smudge herbs, strengthen your identity, and empower and endow yourself with courage and determination. This is most potent on your birth date and time (if known). It is also especially effective during the Sun-sign period. You can, however, use your zodiacal smudge at any time during the year when you feel undermined or need an additional boost of self-confidence.

☉ Sunday

The day of the Sun is for rituals for personal fulfilment and ambition, power and success, and self-confidence. It is for asserting or strengthening your identity and individuality, for innovation of all kinds and new beginnings, for bringing health and prosperity after illness or misfortune and for breaking a run of bad luck.

Herbs and incenses: Bay, cinnamon, white sage, frankincense, juniper, rosemary.

☽ Monday

The day of the Moon is for rituals concerning the home and family. In particular, it is for all women's concerns, children, animals, fertility and protection especially while travelling and against psychic attack, psychic development, clairvoyance, meaningful dreams and healing.

Herbs and incenses: Chamomile, grey sage, jasmine, lotus, myrrh, mimosa and wintergreen. I would also add sweetgrass, as it is a Mother Goddess herb and is quite magical when smudged under a full Moon.

♂ Tuesday

The day of Mars is for courage and change, independence, taking the initiative, standing out against injustice and protecting the vulnerable and loved ones under threat. It is also for overcoming seemingly impossible odds and for physical health, passion and virility.

Herbs and incenses: Basil, cypress, dragon's blood, ginger, mint, pine and thyme.

☿ Wednesday

The day of Mercury is for money-making ventures, for improving memory and sharpening logic, for learning, examinations and tests, and for mastering new technology. It is also for short-distance or brief holidays, business negotiations, overcoming debts, and repelling envy, malice and spite and those who would deceive.

Herbs and incenses: Dill, fennel, lavender, lemongrass, parsley and valerian.

♃ Thursday

The day of Jupiter is for increasing what already exists, so it can bring greater prosperity and abundance. This includes improving fortune and career prospects, and obtaining promotion or building on what you have already achieved. It is for leadership, creativity, idealism, justice and matters of the law, marriage, permanent relationships (business and personal) and for trustworthiness and fidelity in these.

Herbs and incenses: Cedar, cloves, hyssop, mistletoe, sage (not sagebrush) and sandalwood.

♀ Friday

The day of Venus is associated with love and all forms of love magic, especially to attract love. It is for beauty, the arts, crafts and music, relationships, friendships, blossoming sexuality, the slow but sure growth of prosperity, and all environmental concerns; also, like the Moon, Venus brings fertility and oversees women's health matters.

Herbs and incenses: Apple, geranium, mugwort, rose, strawberry, vervain.

♄ Saturday

The day of Saturn is for rituals to overcome obstacles that are long-standing or need careful handling, and for matters of financial security and property. It is for lifting depression or doubts, for meditation, mystical experiences, past-life work and long-term psychic protection, for locating lost objects, animals and people, and for regaining self-control, whether over bad habits or emotions.

Herbs and incenses: Gum arabic (acacia gum), cypress, magnolia, orchid, patchouli, tamarisk.

Signs of the zodiac and their smudge herbs and incenses

Aries: 21 March–20 April
Carnation, copal, juniper, mint, pine

Taurus: 21 April–21 May
Apple, lilac, rose, thyme, vervain

Gemini: 22 May–21 June
Almond, lavender, lemongrass, lily of the valley, parsley

Cancer: 22 June–22 July
Eucalyptus, gardenia, jasmine, lemon balm, myrrh

Leo: 23 July–23 August
Bay, cinnamon, frankincense, marigold, rosemary

Virgo: 24 August–22 September
Cypress, fennel, honeysuckle, lavender, lily

Libra: 23 September–23 October
Marjoram, mugwort, strawberry, vanilla, violet

Scorpio: 24 October–22 November
Allspice, basil, cloves, cumin, geranium

Sagittarius: 23 November–21 December
Cedar, ginger, orange, sage, sandalwood

Capricorn: 22 December–20 January
Magnolia, oakmoss, patchouli, vervain, vetivert

Aquarius: 21 January–18 February
Acacia, benzoin, cherry, citron, orchid

Pisces: 19 February–20 March
Lemon, lotus, mimosa, orris root, sweetgrass

A six-herb ritual for empowerment

On page 63, I talked about how each of the six directions in the Native North American world had its own herbs. By combining these in smudging rituals you can generate a great deal of power for an important or urgent venture.

Arrangements for the ritual

You can work within your Medicine Wheel, or visualise or smudge a clockwise circle round yourself. I have suggested herbs for each direction, but there are variations and you can select your own.

* Set a small dish of one of the following herbs at each of the six directions.

   East: Lavender, mint or lemongrass
   South: Bay, chamomile or rosemary
   West: Cedar, rose petals or thyme
   North: Cypress, pine or mugwort
   Centre left: Sage for Father Sky
   Centre right: Sweetgrass for Mother Earth

   You could also burn white sage for Father Sky and grey sage for Mother Earth.

* Set a candle or outdoor torch at each of the directional points. Use the colours I suggest on page 62, i.e. red in the East, yellow in the South, black in the West, white with the North. (These were those used by the Oglala Sioux.) Alternatively, you can use colours according to the Western magical tradition: yellow in the East, red or orange in the South, blue in the West and green or brown in the North.

* Set two candles in the centre, gold for Father Sky on the left and silver for Mother Earth on the right. Alternatively, you may use pure white for both. Place tapers by them, so you can re-light your smudge bowl if necessary.

  Carry out this and the candle lighting in silence.

* Light each of the candles in turn, asking each for the blessing of its sacred animal: the Hawk in the East, the Stag in the South, the Salmon in the West, the Bear in the North, the Eagle soaring above the centre and the Buffalo for Mother Earth at the foot of the central invisible World Tree.

* Standing in the centre of your Medicine Wheel or the candle circle, light a third of a bowl of white sage for Father Sky. This will form your nucleus smudge. As you fan it, say:

  Father Sky, mighty Eagle, make my spirit soar.

* Move to the East and create a circle of smoke around the Medicine Wheel or circle, embracing all the compass points within it, saying:

  May the circle that is cast remain unbroken.

* Still standing in the East, face outwards. Take just a few lavender seeds and add them to the smudge bowl and fan the smoke upwards. They should burn as the sage will be hot enough to smoulder them, but do not add too many. Say:

  Father Sky, mighty Eagle, Hawk of vision, make my spirit soar.

* Move to the South and add three or four bay leaves to the bowl – it will flare up. Fan the smoke in the bowl and say:

  Mighty Eagle, Hawk of vision, Stag of strength, make my spirit soar.

* Carry the bowl to the West, re-lighting or adding more sage if necessary, to maintain the smoke flare. Add a handful of cedar, saying:

Mighty Eagle, Hawk of vision, Stag of strength, wise Salmon mother, make my spirit soar.

* Go to the North and add to the bowl a small brush of pine needles, saying:

Mighty Eagle, Hawk of vision, Stag of strength, wise Salmon mother, noble Bear, make my spirit soar.

* Move finally to the centre right and add some shavings from a sweetgrass braid to the bowl, saying:

Buffalo, bringer of abundance, Mother, to all these sacred creatures I add your love and protection. Keep me rooted as my spirit soars

* Stand in the centre and smudge yourself upwards from feet to crown, ending with a triple clockwise circle, saying:

Thus do I aspire, thus seek the power to move forward in this my endeavour. Blessings be.

* Sit quietly and watch the smoke rising gently and the candles burning around you, and know you are connected with Sky and Earth and all the directions of the sacred hoop of existence and so will never be alone.

Smudging and rites of passage

Many people hold smudging ceremonies at significant points in their lives, either as part of a ceremony, whether joyous or sad, or as a private way of expressing their own feelings and making the occasion sacred. This is especially so if you find a formal ceremony does not meet your own needs, or if you need to mourn alone.

Gary, who grows and sells smudging herbs in Australia, wrote to me about the joining ceremony that was held with his partner Dee:

The most memorable result of smudging I can recall, was at our joining ceremony in September 1999. The ceremony was timed to commence at Moonrise, approximately 7.30 pm. It was a full Moon.

The setting was a grassed terrace cut into the hillside between our house and the house-dam (we are on a farm), with floating candles on the dam, a large iron candelabra with candles for light to read by and three braziers, one with a fire burning and the other two containing lit charcoal. These two were strategically placed to take advantage of the very pleasant easterly breeze that had graced us with its presence for the evening, and placed alongside each of them was a basket containing a mix of various smudging herbs. The stage was set! Our guests had been invited to arrive at 5 pm and were offered hors d'oeuvres and refreshments to sustain them while they were re-acquainted or got to know each other. Their combined energy as the time approached to move down to witness our joining was, as anticipated, high. As the Moon rose, we took our places along with the celebrant, our chosen witnesses and our two lovely 16-year-old twin girls, one at each of the braziers with the herbs. Everyone else was then asked to move into position just above and downwind of us. As they did so the twins began to sprinkle herbs on to the coals. The result was nothing short of amazing. Aided by the breeze, a mass smudging took place, the effect being very calming on all present. Chatter reduced to a murmur, then silence. A wonderful mood had been set.

Needless to say, every following moment flowed beautifully, supported by further applications of herbs to the coals. It was a truly joyous occasion followed by an incredibly sumptuous supper. Smudge is in daily use at our home/workplace. We find it supports the love and integrity in what we do.

I also received an account of smudging from a woman who had returned home after the funeral of her very dear schoolfriend, Esme. Jan had hardly known anyone at the funeral and had felt very isolated. She told me:

I sat in the dark overlooking the garden and I felt that the day was incomplete for me and that the service, according to a faith that I found hard to understand, had not answered any of my own needs to say goodbye. I lit a dark candle and then a bowl of sweetgrass braids and I sat watching the smoke curling upwards, thinking of our childhood in the countryside, of Esme running through the fields, of all our grandiose plans woven as we climbed high in the apple tree, how our lives had taken very different paths. I spoke all the words I had never had time to say on to the rising smoke, of my gratitude for our time together and all the kindness she had shown me, of my regrets for the way we had inevitably moved apart in recent years. As I spoke, I was aware of her presence, though I saw nothing, only a sense that she had heard and that our friendship was now complete.

Chapter 10
Smudging and Psychic Development

When I was a child, smoke was part of my magical life in the industrial Midlands. This may not have been quite as exotic as smoke rising across the plains of the American Midwest, but it served the same function psychically to awaken the inner imagery system that is a direct guide to unconscious wisdom.

We had a coal fire and I could always tell if anyone was at home when I came from school in the winter by whether there was smoke coming out of the chimney. I would sit on winter evenings watching the changing pictures in the world of the Fire fairies in the grate, dropping paper wishes into the embers to be carried on the smoke up the chimney. Each of the factory chimneys had its distinct smoke pattern that created images in the early morning sky. To me they were dragons, the faces of genies or witches on broomsticks, and I knew if I saw the smiling wizard that came out of the Corporation Yard's very un-environmentally friendly stack that it would be a good day at school.

Years later, when I first encountered smoke magic, I was struggling to interpret the images. Then I suddenly realised that in childhood the meanings were so clear. It is only when we move away from childhood that this ability to tap into the universal symbol system recedes. There are many ways you can use smudging as part of your spiritual development but sometimes it is just a question of reconnecting with the wisdom of childhood, in which everything was part of an interconnected universe brilliant with rainbows.

Even if you do not consciously work on evolving psychically, these powers will automatically re-emerge as you make smudging part of your life and through the sacred circle tap once more the magical and healing energies that are not confined to any one time or place.

A ritual for increased psychic awareness

In any psychic work, you can access this deep unconscious wisdom by tapping into any one of your psychic senses. By doing so, you activate all the other psychic abilities that reside just beyond the physical senses. Smoke magic enables you to see psychically images of different times, places and dimensions through the power known as clairvoyance. You also acquire clairaudient abilities so that you can, as you did in childhood, attune to sounds beyond the range of the physical ear.

Most of all, the fragrance of smoke triggers psychometry. This is the power whereby you can evoke from a crystal or artefact not only its own history but also insights about those who have owned or even momentarily held it.

Arrangements for the ritual

Because of the powerful nature of smudging, you do not need elaborate preparations for psychic work as smudging carries in-built protection for exploring other dimensions. The following method is one I find the most helpful with smoke magic. I originally used it with incense sticks but have since discovered that a bowl of smudge herbs works equally well. This is a good ritual to include while you are waiting for charcoal to heat for another purpose, as it opens up the channels of awareness that make any smudging doubly effective.

For increasing psychic awareness, I would suggest either a mixture of three or four frankincense and sandalwood incense sticks in a tall container or incense holder, or a bowl of white or grey sage and mugwort. Alternatively, you can smoulder lavender heads on charcoal. You can use a smudge stick of sage and lavender or sage and rosemary but you will need a safe heatproof container to hold it while you meditate.

* Light a horseshoe of purple candles behind your incense. Alternatively, smudge by the light of the Sun or Moon, so that the smoke from your smudge bowl reflects the light of these heavenly bodies.

* Burn your smudge or incense stick and, using either a fan or the bowl, smudge a circle round yourself, beginning in the East, saying:

  May the circle that is cast remain unbroken. Blessings be.

* Hold between your hands an amethyst or smoky quartz crystal (these will open your natural psychic channels) and raise it slightly so that the smoke swirls round it and you can see the light within it.

* Allow images and words to form in your mind, in the smoke or in the crystal or more likely in all three. Do not attempt to analyse them.

This unstructured time is a good way of tuning in to your intuitive wisdom. You may find that even if you do not want to practise psychic arts formally, your time of contemplation will result in increased intuition and awareness of hidden factors in your everyday world, especially a more heightened sensitivity to people and situations.

Over the weeks, change the fragrances by introducing bay, cedar, jasmine, myrrh and patchouli, rosemary, sweetgrass and thyme. Experiment with these and others and you may find that specific incenses evoke clairvoyance, psychometric abilities or even past-life recall. Note in your smudging journal any that seem especially potent for you; you can then burn these when you need to make an important decision, or when you feel unsettled or in need of inspiration. In time, you may settle on one or two fragrances for spiritual work.

Smoke divination

Smoke divination is one of the oldest forms of decision-making in the world. Like all divination, whether using natural phenomena, the Chinese Book of Changes (I Ching) or Tarot cards, the results that are obtained work by psychokinesis (mind control). In the case of smoke, it answers your question both by its direction and by the images it invokes. This may seem hard to believe, but we scarcely understand the relationship between mind and matter, and time after time these methods do offer an accurate guide to choosing the correct action.

Science is also increasingly demonstrating these connections. One plant energy researcher in America, Marcel Vogel, experimented with children and plants. He instructed the children to move their hands backwards and forwards gently over the leaves. Eventually, the plants began to sway with the movements of the children's hands, although there was no physical contact between the child and the plant and no breeze.

A divination ritual

Work in a room without obvious draughts. If you observe the smoke before and after divination, you may notice that concentrating on an issue does quite dramatically affect the direction it curls. Place a mirror behind the smudge and sit with candles or the light of the Moon or the Sun behind your back – this will help you to see the smoke clearly.

* Light a smudge stick and place it in a secure container. Alternatively, place smudge herbs in a bowl, but initially light only a single stream of smudge in your bowl. You can also use an incense stick in the fragrance related to the issue under question (see pages 138–40 and 166–80).

* As you light the smudge or incense, ask your question either out loud or in your mind.

* Watch the smoke in the mirror placed behind the smudge.

If the smoke goes directly upwards, the answer is positive, whether to act, to speak or to make a change. Your wish will come to fruition soon.

If the smoke turns to the left as it rises upwards, you should seek the help of others to fulfil your plans and they may take a little longer to fulfil than you expected.

If it rises and turns to the right, you will succeed by your own efforts, so do not be deterred by others' doubts or criticisms that may arise out of their fear of change rather than real concerns.

If the smoke forms circles, billows at a low level or goes out, you should wait and ask again in a few days.

If the smoke changes direction rapidly, you should try an alternative means to achieve your desire.

* Light extra streams of smudge or three or four incense sticks close together so the smoke merges. Through half-closed eyes look at the

smoke reflected in the mirror and allow it to suggest images. These may appear in the smoke, in the mirror or in your mind's vision – they all stem from the same process. You may see your image in the context of a scene.

* Note or draw the pictures and relevant thoughts, but accept what you see without trying to second-guess or rationalise their meaning. You are using the intuitive part of your mind that works more like a child's storybook than a psychology manual. But it is no less important than the conscious thought processes, and may provide inspiration when reason fails.

* Close your eyes to reconnect with the wisdom, then open them and blink as you did when viewing auras. You can continue this until you have four or five images. Because you may not have used this visual part of your mind since childhood, it can take practice to get back in touch.

The meanings of the images you may recognise from your dreams and from the symbol system we all carry in our genes that is expressed in myth and fairy tale. However, on page 183 I have suggested books in which you will find symbol meanings if you want to match them up.

If you cannot see any relevance, create a story weaving the symbols in the order you saw them.

Astral projection

When you were healing using shamanic drumming and chanting, you may have experienced the sensation of floating or flying. This is called astral projection, or astral travel. Many people, myself included, believe that we do not physically leave our bodies in such experiences, but that our mind is able to travel spiritually in this light trance state.

It is similar to what happens in dreams and daytime visions, when we can not only see people whom we know in our everyday world, but also visit other lands and explore the past, the future and even those magical mythological planes of childhood.

The methods I describe below are those I have used successfully with groups in Sweden, beginning the process of astral projection in the imagination and passing by easy stages to psychic awareness whereby the soul flows and expands rather than leaves the body.

A ritual for astral travel

In our more significant dreams, and in astral travel, we experience colours that are richer and flowers that are more fragrant than in everyday life. We meet loved ones who may have died or living people we may never encounter in life, but who may share with us our dream drama and may offer us wise counsel or reassurance.

* Light a bowl of mugwort or thyme with sage, frankincense, jasmine or sandalwood granules on charcoal or frankincense or three or four sandalwood incense sticks in a horseshoe on a table.

* Position a lamp (fibre-optics are excellent) or a purple candle in a broad-based holder on a shelf, or if you have wall lights switch on one as a focus. Place your smudge either on a low table, if you are sitting on the floor, or in front of you at a safe distance. It should be at approximately a 60-degree angle to the higher-level light source.

* Half-close your eyes and visualise a spiral staircase in the smoke, surrounded by fragrant flowers.

* Slowly ascend it in your mind's vision, moving closer and closer to the light, in which a doorway opens. When you have reached the doorway, you will see it open into another radiant world and that the pathway of fragrance continues.
* If you prefer, just look through it for as long as you want and then descend once more.
* Alternatively, if you wish, pass through the doorway, where you will be greeted by a guide. It may be someone you recognise from your dreams, an angel or a wise figure from mythology.
* He or she will guide you along the perfumed path, perhaps into a world where there are talking animals, friendly dragons, fairies, magical castles and alchemists. If anything seems frightening, remember you have your guardian with you. Simply breathe deeply and the fragrance will melt away any fears. But also remember that this is an experience coming from deep in your psyche and what may at first seem to be a foe can if confronted or questioned lose its negative aspects and even offer you strengths.
* You can at any time return by counting down from 10 to 1, but there usually comes a point when you are aware that the world is

beginning to fade and you can retrace your steps along the fragrant path to the light doorway. Pause and ask your guardian if she or he has a message for you. Then begin the descent down the smoke spiral, sitting quietly in the light and allowing impressions to ebb and flow and contemplating the message of the guardian.

* Even if you did not go through the doorway, you may still have glimpsed through it a rich scene with many images that can be developed as the smoke wafts gently over you.

In future astral work you will find that your conscious visualisation is gradually replaced by spontaneous connection and each time you pass through the doorway your guide will lead you along different paths of discovery and the messages may become more complex.

Experiment with different fragrances and light sources.

A past-life ritual

In your astral world you may have already glimpsed scenes from past centuries as well as different lands, perhaps identified with characters or events you saw. Increasingly people in the western world are coming to the conclusion, long-held in many eastern religions, that we do have recall of past lives. There is controversy over whether these are actual lives we have experienced personally or whether we are tapping into the cosmic memory bank for images that mirror our own present situation.

Whatever the reality, past-life recall can offer solutions to current dilemmas and may provide healing for fears or traumas whose cause seems elusive. Bay leaves, mimosa, myrrh, orris root, rose, sage and thyme are all good for past-life recall and you can burn herbs or incense either as granules or as sticks.

Arrangements for the ritual

Set up your light source as for the astral projection ritual on page 160.

* Ascend a spiral stairway of smoke, but this time create a shadowy doorway leading to a tunnel that goes from the light along rough-hewn copper or stone walls, glinting with jewels, to a distant point of light. The fragrance will still be with you and, if you feel uncertain, pause and inhale deeply for a moment. You need not be afraid because a few steps ahead is your guide, who will turn and smile.

* This time you will see the tunnel becoming lighter and brighter and soon you will be in daylight in a lovely wood.

* Continue to follow your guide and the fragrance, and when you see a building enter it and observe the scene. You may rapidly identify with one of the characters, but though you can see and hear everything quite clearly you are invisible and nothing can harm you. You may move to other places and may witness events or dialogue that mirror and explain or resolve issues in your current life.

* As before, you can return at any time to the everyday world by counting from 10 to 1. But you will probably find that the experience draws to a natural resolution and your guide will take you back down the tunnel to the fragrant smoke stairway. Again she or he may offer a wise message.

* While you can carry out astral projection as part of your smudge work about once a week, past-life work should be confined to whenever you feel the need. It tends not to be so effective more than once a month unless you are undergoing a major change period. In this case you may return to the same period several times.

Chapter 11
Herbs and incenses for smudging

This chapter contains a list of most of the common herbs you may want to use for smudging. All can also be obtained as combustible incense in sticks or cones and this is often a good way to try them out first, to see whether you like the fragrance and if it is effective magically for you.

The more resinous herbs can also be found either as prepared incense granules or as part of an incense mix and I have listed some suppliers on pages 184–7. But there are many other outlets, such as New Age stores and mail order companies. Consult a number of sources and you will find herbs you may need, such as benzoin, copal, dragon's blood, gum arabic (acacia gum), myrrh and sandalwood.

Noting the properties of your herbs

There are many variations in the fragrance and burning power of herbs, even within the same species, depending on such factors as soil, climate and even the way they are dried. There really is no substitute for experimentation, so you may enjoy seeking out herbs to burn, and making notes on the results. If you are a keen gardener or botanist, you can look up the Latin generic names in a book or on the internet and this can be very useful, especially for ordering by mail order and for consistency.

However, the majority of smudgers focus on materials found easily to hand and just keep simple, working notes. When you buy a new culinary herb, try it in a bowl and on charcoal and note the differences. Use dead leaves, bark and fallen, browning flower petals. Before many months have passed, you will have a whole range in your notebook. In such a case your smudge journal might consist of entries such as:

> *Juniper – at the end of the garden – good on charcoal but not in smudge sticks. Brilliant after quarrels, but can cause irritability if burned to lift inertia.*

With further investigation, you may find that your particular bush or tree possesses those qualities, but a commercial juniper incense stick has a different effect. Even this can vary between brands.

You may also find that a local species of herbs works particularly well for some purpose. For example, the pine that grows near my caravan seems to smudge well as a stick, but I have found that other kinds of fir and pine, even from the opposite side of the caravan site, need charcoal. Native North Americans and other indigenous peoples gleaned this knowledge not only from experience and intuition, but also by merging spiritually with the essence of each herb.

As you work with smudge and allow your natural affinities to develop, you will instinctively become able to tell in advance if a specific plant will be better for smudging than the one in the pot next to it in the garden centre. If in doubt, hold your pendulum over several pots of herbs in turn, asking it to indicate the one that is right for smudging. This may be shown by heaviness, almost a pull of gravity, or by the pendulum circling clockwise. Small children will unerringly tell you the best herbs or even incense sticks to use for a particular purpose, precisely because they do not know what the properties *ought* to be. As you work more with smudging, so you may move away from the rules and knowledge of how things ought to be, back into the instinctive knowledge of nature and healing that we all possess.

Herbs and their properties

Below I have listed 65 herbs and their traditional magical properties, but you may discover additional and alternative ones that work for you. If you do find a reference to an unfamiliar flower or herb, for example in an astrological list, you can be sure that the properties will be similar to those of more familiar ones under the same ruling sign or planet. So, for example, cherry blossom, which is ruled by Venus, will be similar to apple blossom. I have listed herb books on page 182 that include more comprehensive lists.

Allspice: Brings healing of all kinds, but it primarily endows prosperity, strength, change and passion.
  Ruled by Mars.
Apple blossom: Promotes love, fertility, optimism, inner beauty and youthfulness. It is also used in rituals concerning babies and children.
  Ruled by Venus.

Avocado: Increases desire and an awareness of beauty in self or in the environment. It can therefore be used in Earth conservation and other green rituals.

Ruled by Venus.

Basil: Reduces stress and clears the mind. It removes toxins, so is also good for anti-pollution rituals. Basil is a herb of love and fidelity and also attracts abundance and prosperity. It is good for overcoming fears of flying.

Ruled by Mars.

Bay: Brings psychic protection and the healing of sorrow. It purifies all forms of pollution and negativity, endows strength and endurance, brings prosperity and, as the herb of marriage, encourages fidelity. It is good for past-life work.

Ruled by the Sun.

Benzoin: Melts away stress, tension, anger, resentment, emotional pain and frustrations. As a positive influence, benzoin increases self-confidence and attracts prosperity, both material and spiritual, and improves concentration.

Ruled by the Sun.

Carnation: A herb of protection used in healing rituals to give strength and to trigger the immune system. It is also a herb of family devotion and happiness.

Ruled by Jupiter.

Cedar: A traditional Native North American smudge that brings both cleansing and healing. Cedar is a herb of purification and protection, guarding the home against all negative influences and the person against dark thoughts.

Ruled by Jupiter and the Sun.

Chamomile: The children's herb, also known as the oil of kindness, chamomile is effective for every childhood problem, including hyperactivity, general restlessness and sleeplessness – and for adults with similar problems. Chamomile brings gradual increase of money, affection, friendship and family unity. It is also very protective.

Ruled by the Sun.

Cinnamon: A bringer of money and success, it is also a herb of love and passion. A third area it rules is healing and it is potent in increasing psychic awareness and offering protection.

Ruled by Mars.

Cloves: Prevent gossip, malice and envy and help in acquiring new skills, partly because they improve memory. A natural aphrodisiac, cloves both attract love and awaken sexual feelings. For those who have suffered loss, cloves offer comfort. They also bring money.

Ruled by Jupiter.

Copal: Burned as smudge incense in Central and South America, endowing protection and attracting love. It clears negativity from people, artefacts and places and is especially good for cleansing crystals.

Ruled by Mars and the Sun.

Cypress: Brings consolation after sorrow or loss, bringing acceptance and helping to let go of grief and to move forward. It brings wisdom, understanding and compassion towards the distress of self and others. It is a herb of healing and protection.

Ruled by Saturn.

Dragon's blood: A very powerful incense, dragon's blood is associated with the increase of passion and especially male potency. It also attracts love and brings back faithless lovers (if you want them). It is very protective, acting as a shield against negativity to place and person.

Ruled by Mars.

Eucalyptus: This is a herb of purification of mind, body and soul, driving out negativity and anger, as well as repelling deliberate psychological and psychic attack. Eucalyptus will provide the impetus for action and decisions, especially when people and projects have reached an impasse. It offers clear focus and increased concentration.

Ruled by the Moon.

Fennel: From Roman times, fennel has been regarded as a herb of courage, stamina, renewed strength and energy. It improves mental alertness and also brings protection from unwanted visitors and all forms of external hostility. In its gentler aspects it protects babies, young children and new mothers.

Ruled by Mercury.

Ferns: These are initiators of change, travel of all kinds and fertility; they can bring or reveal ways to unexpected prosperity, usually through the expression of untapped potential. They are traditionally associated with rain-making and midsummer wealth spells.

Ruled by Mercury.

Figs: Powerful for both male and female fertility and potency and for attracting prosperity and abundance in all forms and areas of life. Figs are also associated with creativity and the acquisition of wisdom and are bringers of harmony both within the self and with others. Figs are increasingly popular as an incense in the domestic as well as the magical world.

Ruled by Jupiter.

Frankincense: Regarded as the most noble of incenses, used in ceremonies and formal celebrations throughout the ages and in many cultures, a gift from the deities, bringing healing and power. It offers confidence to aim high, attracting abundance of all kinds, money and success. It also grants access to higher dimensions through psychic work and contact with angels and spirit guides. Use it for astral projection and also past-life work.

Ruled by the Sun.

Freesia: A herb for increasing trust, especially after loss or betrayal, that brings belief in a better tomorrow. It increases self-esteem and is a good herb to deflect harshness or undue criticism.

Ruled by the Moon.

Geranium: A herb of harmony, restoring peace and well-being to the home or workplace, and encouraging positive, non-confrontational interactions. It can reconcile those who are estranged and melt away emotional coldness, rigidity and indifference in encounters. It relieves tension, depression, doubts and despair, replacing them with gentle optimism.

Ruled by Venus.

Ginger: Much prized in the East and still used in China to aid potency and ensure long life. In the Indian Ayurvedic tradition it is called the universal healer. Ginger offers protection when travelling and attracts money, success and passion, and also love. It is a physical and emotional energiser.

Ruled by Mars.

Gum arabic (acacia gum): This is a powerful protector against physical and psychic harm. It is good in an incense mix with sandalwood, frankincense or myrrh for all forms of psychic development, stimulating prophetic dreams. It also brings money and platonic love.

Ruled by the Sun.

Heather: A herb associated with passion, fidelity in love and the bringing of good fortune. Offers empowerment and maximises opportunities and is especially potent at midsummer. It is traditionally linked with weather magic, especially rain-making.

Ruled by Venus.

Honeysuckle: A natural luck-bringer, it offers a steady increase in prosperity, being especially potent for breaking a run of misfortune. It enhances psychic awareness and is deeply protective.

Ruled by Jupiter.

Hyacinth: Potent in overcoming opposition in love, and in bringing happiness and reconciliation where there has been estrangement. It also drives away nightmares.

Ruled by Venus.

Hyssop: From the Hebrew world, this herb is mentioned many times in the Bible for its ability to cleanse the body of illness. Hyssop is primarily a herb of purification, banishing sad thoughts, stress, despair and doubts and leaving a positive approach. It removes negativity from the home and from objects that have unhappy associations or that have belonged to people who were unhappy. It also protects against psychic attack.

Ruled by Jupiter.

Ivy: Known as the Queen of Yule, whose partner was the Holly King. It is a symbol of fidelity and married love, of permanent relationships and also of joy. Ivy drives away negativity and is protective, especially for women. I find ivy incense sticks are best for smudging.

Ruled by Saturn.

Jasmine: Potent for all Moon magic, especially on the crescent and the night of the full Moon. It induces prophetic dreams and is used for many aspects of psychic development, especially astral projection. Jasmine is a herb of love and gives it a spiritual dimension.

Ruled by the Moon.

Juniper: A very protective herb, keeping people, animals and property safe from theft, vandalism and psychic attacks as well as illness. It is a natural purifier for the home against past negative influences and future misfortune, especially at New Year and for house moves. It also increases male potency.

Ruled by the Sun.

Lavender: An all-purpose healing herb, gently cleansing and empowering. It promises a gradual and gentle improvement in health and well-being, inducing peaceful sleep. In a room it will encourage gentle, positive interactions and reduce hyperactivity in children. Lavender is the herb of love and, especially for women, it attracts gentle and kind lovers. It is also good for wish magic.

Ruled by Mercury.

Lemon: The breath of life, offering energy, clarity, logic and integrity. It is also a light-bringer, cutting though secrecy, doubt and dishonesty and cleansing atmospheres and attitudes.

Ruled by the Moon.

Lemongrass: Clears away negative emotions among family, friends or colleagues, past resentment and feuds from the past that no longer serve any purpose. It also removes painful memories and helps to leave behind destructive relationships; lemongrass also enhances psychic awareness.

Ruled by Mercury.

Lemon verbena: Excellent for breaking a run of bad luck in your life and gradually restoring positivity. It also cleanses both places and property, preventing darker energies from entering. It is potent in love rituals, especially for increasing self-love and self-esteem.

Ruled by Mercury.

Lilac: Brings joy and harmony to all domestic matters, cleansing all negativity and anxiety. It is especially good for smudging boundaries to keep away all malevolence and in houses in which poltergeist activity is disturbing. Lilac also helps with the acceptance of the frailty of self and others.

Ruled by Venus.

Lily: Associated with the Virgin Mary. A natural purifier that breaks negative influences in love and lessens the hold of addictions and obsessions. It is also sacred to the Mother Goddess and so is used as an incense in all goddess magic.

Ruled by the Moon.

Lily of the valley: A herb of gentle optimism, bringing light and hope even into seemingly impossible situations. It also sharpens mental faculties and improves memory.

Ruled by Mercury.

Marigold: Increases positivity in the home, makes a lover more affectionate, promotes fidelity and helps in all legal problems. It also brings prophetic dreams and is good for divinatory work. Marigold attracts luck and prosperity.

Ruled by the Sun.

Mimosa: A herb of the night, associated with secrets and secret love. It brings love and friendship especially for older people. Mimosa calms anxiety and over-sensitivity to criticism and brings harmony and happiness, melting away opposition and hostility. It is good for past-life recall.

Ruled by Saturn.

Mint: A healing and purifying herb, effective at home and in sickrooms to drive away all negativity and illness. It offers protection against illness, accident, hostility and theft or damage to the home, and also attracts money. In small quantities, combined with gentle herbs such as chamomile, it can help to relieve insomnia and whirling thoughts.

Ruled by Mercury.

Mistletoe: Known to the Druids as the all-healer, mistletoe, especially in incense stick form, is effective for healing sorrows, increasing male potency, overcoming injustice and finding what is lost. It can also be part of healing rituals, whether for a person, an animal, a place or the planet.

Ruled by Jupiter.

Moss: A natural bringer of good luck and prosperity that can be used for rituals where permanence is desired, whether in jobs or relationships. Water magic and divination are also enhanced by burning this herb, as are all green rituals. It is best in the form of incense sticks.

Ruled by the Moon.

Mugwort: The herb of psychic awareness, for divination and astral projection. It is also deeply protective against all physical and psychic harm and fears. Mugwort increases desire and fertility.

Ruled by Venus.

Myrrh: One of the oldest protective and purification herbs, associated with the healing of the mind and spirit as well as the body. It is a good herb to burn as incense for protection and for healing. Myrrh promotes higher states of consciousness and so is good for all spiritual work, especially for recalling past lives.

Ruled by the Moon.

Myrtle: Sometimes called the woman's herb, since it is especially lucky and protective if planted by women. It may be mixed with other fragrances, and is potent for all fidelity and love rituals, especially those concerning marriage or mature love. Myrtle is also effective for property matters and all aspects of security.

Ruled by Venus.

Neroli: *see* Orange blossom

Nutmeg: A herb of fertility and also healing, especially of the environment. It also promotes the gradual increase of wealth and is a luck-bringer. It shares many properties with almond.

Ruled by the Moon.

Orange blossom (neroli): This is a symbol of marriage, committed relationships, fidelity and fertility. Neroli increases self-esteem and self-love and encourages optimism. It prevents mood swings, crises of confidence and panic attacks. Neroli also restores trust after betrayal.

Ruled by the Sun.

Orris root: Increases psychic awareness and is especially potent for past-life work. It also brings love and drives away all negativity.

Ruled by Venus.

Parsley: A divinatory herb with a subtle fragrance, parsley is said to encourage fertility, love and passion and is protective against psychological or psychic attack. It should be planted on Good Friday, the day on which evil is said to hold no sway. It is also used in anti-pollution and environmental rituals.

Ruled by Mercury.

Patchouli: Associated with prosperity and used to bring employment and increase business opportunities. It is also frequently used in ceremonies to heal the planet, as it is a natural restorer of balance. Patchouli is a fertility herb and increases sensual attraction.

Ruled by Saturn.

Pine: A purifier of all forms of negativity, hostile atmospheres and dishonesty, protective especially against emotional blackmail. It offers courage and perseverance under difficulty, strengthening integrity and clear focus. Pine is effective against all kinds of malice as it returns hostility to the sender. It is a natural healer. Piñon pine needs charcoal to help it burn.

Ruled by Mars.

Rose: Like lavender, rose is a natural healer and restorer of well-being on the physical, emotional and spiritual planes. Roses have since time immemorial been used in love rituals, to bring dreams of a future lover, to attract love and preserve it. Rose is potent for past-life recall.

Ruled by Venus.

Rosemary: Improves memory, focuses thoughts and increases energy levels. Rosemary, or elf leaf, is also a herb of protection, driving away bad dreams. It is, however, primarily associated with love and passion. Known as the herb of remembrance, especially of love, rosemary can bring about reconciliation. Burn for psychic and especially divinatory work.

Ruled by the Sun.

Sage: Desert grey sage and California white sage are traditional smudge materials, cleansing, healing, protecting and empowering, and can be used in any kind of ritual. They share properties with the many varieties of culinary sage, which can also be burned. These strengths include good health, enhanced wisdom, fertility and long life. Sage in all its forms is a potent herb for developing psychic awareness, allowing glimpses of past and future, astral projection and past-life recall.

Most sages are ruled by Jupiter, though the Desert and California sages are ruled by the Moon and the Sun respectively.

Sandalwood: An ancient ceremonial herb, so its prime focus is in increasing spiritual awareness, offering a path to make contact with the higher self and the spirit guides. It may be used in all psychic and divinatory work, including astral projection and past-life recall. It also heightens meditative abilities.

Ruled by Jupiter and the Moon.

Strawberry: The herb of innocent love, friendship and happiness. It is especially fortunate for adolescent girls, pregnant or new mothers, babies and children, but is also a general luck-bringer.

Ruled by Venus.

Sweetgrass: A traditional Native North American smudge, bringing healing, gentle empowerment, beauty and harmony and, above all, abundance in all its forms.

Ruled by the Moon.

Thyme: A powerful divinatory herb that stimulates prophetic dreams, astral projection and past-life work. It is a health-bringer, improving memory and mental abilities, and giving courage and strength.

Ruled by Venus.

Vanilla: A herb of love, especially lasting love, and so is burned in fidelity rituals. It also brings an increase of passion and sexual magnetism. Vanilla increases mental acuity and is a natural energiser.

Ruled by Venus.

Vervain: Offers protection against all negativity for people, animals and the home. It is especially protective for young children and drives away any night terror. Vervain is also used for naming ceremonies for babies. It is a symbol of truth and fidelity particularly in love and close friendship.

Ruled by Venus.

Vetivert: Will break a period of bad luck in love and can attract people who will bring happiness. It repels all who would interfere in and destroy a loving relationship. Vetivert also attracts prosperity and protects possessions and property from theft and vandalism, so is potent as part of a boundary smudge.

Ruled by Saturn.

Violet: Gently clears confused thoughts and emotion. It is mildly protective and will attract love and increase desire, especially if mixed with lavender. Violet will also reverse bad fortune and restore optimism. It can be used in wish-magic.

Ruled by Venus.

Wintergreen: Especially protective of children and sometimes burned at naming ceremonies to endow a child with health and good fortune. It is very protective and brings healing.

Wintergreen is also used in channelling wisdom from higher sources, such as angels.

Ruled by the Moon.

Yarrow: A herb of enduring love and fidelity especially in marriage. Yarrow also repels hostility, banishes fear and wards off sickness. It aids psychic awareness and divination.

Ruled by Venus.

Yerba santa: A very ancient smudge herb, said to encourage reconnection to nature and to the instinctive awareness within us all. It also increases psychic powers, inner radiance and self-esteem. A powerful herb in healing rituals, it brings the courage to overcome any opposition.

Ruled by Jupiter.

Further reading

Smudging and Native North American spirituality

Alexander, Jane, *Smudging and Blessings Pack,* 1998, Sterling, New York

Andrews, Lynne V, *Medicine Woman,* 1991, Arkana

Andrews, Lynne V, *Flight of the Seventh Moon,* 1992, Arkana

Kavasch, E Barrie, and Baar, Karen, *American Indian Healing Arts: Herbs, Rituals and Remedies for Every Season of Life,* 2000, Thorsons

Meadows, Kenneth, *Earth Medicine,* 1995, Element

Moondance, Wolf, *Spirit Medicine,* 1995, Sterling, New York

Wakpski, Diane, *Smudging,* 1996, Black Sparrow Press, US

Healing, auras and chakras

Brennan, Barbara Ann, *Hands of Light: a Guide to Healing Through the Human Energy Field,* 1987, Bantam, New York

Eason, Cassandra, *Aura Reading,* 2000, Piatkus

Eason, Cassandra, *Chakra Power for Healing and Harmony,* 2001, Foulsham

Eden, Donna, *Energy Medicine,* 1999, Piatkus

Herbs and incenses

Cruden, Loren, *Medicine Grove, A Shamanic Herbal,* 1997, Inner Traditions

Culpeper, N, *Culpeper's Colour Herbal,* 1983, Foulsham

Cunningham, Scott, *The Complete Book of Oils, Incenses and Brews,* 1991, Llewellyn, St Paul, Minnesota

Cunningham, Scott, *The Encyclopedia of Magical Herbs,* 1987, Llewellyn, St Paul, Minnesota

Dunwich, Gerena, *Wicca Garden, a Witch's Guide to Magical and Enchanted Herbs and Plants,* 1996, Citadel (Carol), New York

Kollerstrom, Nick, *Gardening and Planting by the Moon,* 2001, Foulsham

Lipp, Frank J, *Herbalism,* 1996, Macmillan

Tompkins and Bird, *The Secret Life of Plants,* 1974, Avon Books, New York

Worwood, Valerie Ann, *The Fragrant Pharmacy,* 1996, Bantam, New York

Shamanism

Devereux, Paul, *Shamanism and the Mystery Lines,* 2000, Foulsham

Johnson, Buffie, *The Lady of the Beasts, Ancient Images of the Goddess and Her Sacred Animals,* 1988, Harper & Row, San Francisco

Johnson, Kenneth, *North Star Road,* 1996, Llewellyn, St Paul, Minnesota

Wahoo, Dhyani, *Voices of Our Ancestors,* 1987, Shambhala

Symbol systems and divination

Eason, Cassandra, *The Complete Guide to Divination*, 1998, Piatkus
Eason, Cassandra, *Crystals Talk to the Woman Within*, 2000, Foulsham
Eason, Cassandra, *Runes Talk to the Woman Within*, 2000, Foulsham
Eason, Cassandra, *Tarot Talks to the Woman Within*, 2000, Foulsham
Fenton, Sasha, *Fortune Telling by Tea Leaves*, 1995, Diamond Books

Psychic protection

Bloom, William, *Psychic Protection*, 1998, Piatkus
Eason, Cassandra, *Psychic Protection Lifts the Spirit*, 2000, Foulsham
Fortune, Dion, *Psychic Self-defence*, 1991, Society of the Inner Light

Useful addresses

Smudging equipment, smudge sticks, smudge herbs, incense, tools, etc.

Australia
Eartharomas Earthcraft
Magpie Flats Herb Farm
273/295 Boyle Road
Kenilworth
Queensland 4574

UK
Dreamcatcher Trading
47 Bruce Road
Sheffield
South Yorkshire
S11 8QD

US
Arizona Gateway Trading Post
Mail-HC 37
Box 919-UPS 14265
N Hiway 93
Golden Valley
AZ 86413

The Cherokee Mall
PO Box 310
Paulden
AZ 86334

Red Eagle Creations
PO Box 451902
Garland
TX 75045-1902

Crystals, candles, magical supplies

Australia
Future Pastimes
24a Collins Street
Kiama
New South Wales

Mysterys
Level 1
314–322 Darling Street
Balmain
New South Wales

The Mystic Trader
125 Flinders Lane
Melbourne 3000

South Africa
The Wellstead
1 Wellington Avenue
Wynberg
Cape 7300

UK
Futhark
18 Halifax Road
Todmorden
Lancs
OL14 5AD

Mandragora
Essex House
Thame
OX9 3LS

Mysteries
7 Monmouth Street
London
WC2H 9DA

Pentagram
11 Cheapside
Wakefield
WF1 2SD

US
The Crystal Cave
415 West Foothill Blvd
Claremont
CA 91711

Eye of the Cat
3314 East Broadway
Long Beach
CA 90803

Open Door Metaphysical
   Shoppe
428 North Buchanan Circle
Suite 16
Pacheco
CA 94553

Spirit Search Emporium
Sun Angel Innovations
3939 W Windmills Blvd
2060 Chandler
AZ 85226

Flower and tree essences

Australia
The Australian Flower Remedy
Society
PO Box 531
Spit Junction
New South Wales 2007

Australian Tree Essences
Sabian
PO Box 527
Kew
Victoria 3101

The Sabian Centre
11 Selbourne Road
Kew
Victoria 31031

Canada
Pacific Essences
PO Box 8317
Victoria
V8W 3R9

UK
Bach Flower Remedies
Healing Herbs Ltd
PO Box 65
Hereford
HR2 0UW

US
Alaskan Flower Essence Project
PO Box 1329
Homer
AL 99603

Desert Alchemy
PO Box 44189
Tucson
AZ 85733

Herbs

UK
Gerard House
736 Christchurch Road
Bournemouth
BH7 6BZ

US
Planet Herbs
815 2nd Avenue
Marlinton
WV 24954

Incenses, specialist

US
Tibetan Incense Company
53 South 200 East
Kanab
UT 84741

Meditation, visualisation and shamanic music

Australia
New World Productions
PO Box 244 WBO
Red Hill
Queensland 4059

UK
Stress Busters
Beechwood Music
Littleton House
Littleton Road
Ashford
Middlesex
TW15 1UU

US
Raven Recordings
744 Broad Street
Room 1815
Newark
NJ 07102

Shamanism

UK
Shamanka
Middle Piccadilly
Hotwell
Dorset
DT9 5LW
(A women's shamanic
empowerment organisation)

Faculty of Shamanics
Kenneth and Beryl Meadows
PO Box 300
Potters Bar
Hertfordshire
EN6 4LE

US
Dance of the Deer Foundation
Center for Shamanic Studies
PO Box 699
Soquel
CA 95073

Foundation of Shamanic Studies
PO Box 1939
Mill Valley
CA 94942

Spiritual healing

Australia
Australian Spiritualist
Association
PO Box 248
Canterbury
New South Wales 2193

Canada
Spiritualist Church of Canada
1835 Lawrence Avenue
East Scarborough
Ontario
M1TR 2Y3

UK
British Alliance of Healing
Associations
Mrs Jo Wallace
3 Sandy Lane
Gisleham
Lowestoft
Suffolk
NR33 8EQ

National Federation of Spiritual
   Healers
Old Manor Farm Studio
Church Street
Sunbury on Thames
Middlesex
TW16 6RG

US
World of Light
PO Box 425
Wappingers Falls
NY 12590
(Can send list of healers)

Index